Annette Bindon & Peter Cole

TEACHING DESIGN & TECHNOLOGY

in the Primary Classroom

Nelson Blackie

TEACHING DESIGN & TECHNOLOGY

in the Primary Classroom

Thomas Nelson and Sons Ltd
Nelson House, Mayfield Road
Walton-on-Thames, Surrey
KT12 5PL, UK

First published by Blackie and Son Ltd 1992
ISBN 0 216 93180 0
© Annette Bindon and Peter Cole

This edition published by Thomas Nelson and Sons Ltd 1992
ISBN 0 17 4233485
NPN 9 8 7 6 5 4 3 2

British Library Cataloguing-in-Publication Data
A catalogue record for this book is available from
the British Library

Printed in Great Britain by Bell & Bain Ltd, Glasgow, Scotland

CONTENTS

INTRODUCTION

This book is intended for primary classroom teachers to help them as they implement the National Curriculum Order for Technology.

We shall be concentrating on the design and technology profile component, which is concerned with developing design and technology capability. The philosophical issues and practical problems will be addressed, with reference to examples of activities which develop capability through the designing and making of artefacts, systems and environments.

The text is organised into four parts:

▶ Part 1 analyses the National Curriculum requirements for design and technology;

▶ Part 2 is concerned with management issues, both organising the children's activities and managing resources;

▶ Part 3 provides an indication of how design and technology can be developed in the classroom and linked with topic work. A resource of ideas for activities is provided by annotated drawings linked in a theme. The ideas are not exclusive to the themes we have chosen and activities can be selected and adapted to fit a much broader range of themes and topics;

▶ Part 4 is divided into ten sections and provides ideas and advice to support your work in design and technology. The contribution of food, textiles and graphics is discussed in three of the sections, and the remaining sections are devoted to construction materials, using energy and controlling children's models.

Part 4 of the book may be used for reference when a problem occurs during a design and technology activity. Children working at Key Stage 2 may also find it useful for reference.

The ideas contained in this book have evolved from our own teaching experience and provide a basis upon which teachers may develop strategies for integrating design and technology into their classroom practice.

The authors are senior lecturers in the Faculty of Education, Nottingham Polytechnic where in-service courses in Technology are run for Primary teachers.

PART ONE

TECHNOLOGY IN THE PRIMARY CURRICULUM

RATIONALE FOR TECHNOLOGY IN THE NATIONAL CURRICULUM

The breadth of technology as defined by the National Curriculum includes all those activities formerly encompassed, in secondary schools, by the departments of home economics, CDT, business studies, art and design, and information technology. The amalgamation of the work of these departments has led to a definition of school technology that includes activities as diverse as creating a wildlife garden, designing and making a meal, producing a newspaper or planning and advertising a school event at which school-made goods may be marketed to raise funds. Although primary schools have generally not divided the curriculum into these separate compartments, technology activities in the primary classroom are just as diverse and varied.

Secondary schools will have to find ways to integrate these different departments into one coherent unit to provide technology education. The integrated approach to the curriculum, characteristic of primary practice, is recommended in the National Curriculum as one through which technological capability may be developed.

The order for technology differentiates between 'design and technology' and 'information technology' and these together comprise 'technology'. It is important to bear this terminology in mind when discussing technology in the National Curriculum because these terms have newly assigned meanings which may not be consistent with previous interpretations.

TECHNOLOGY IN THE NATIONAL CURRICULUM 5 - 16
Two Profile Components

| Design and Technology Capability Attainment Target 1-4 | Information Technology Capability Attainment Target 5 |

Attainment Target 1 - Identifying needs and opportunities
Attainment Target 2 - Generating a design
Attainment Target 3 - Planning and making
Attainment Target 4 - Evaluating

Design and technology activities will usually contain all four attainment targets, but may not always begin with Attainment Target 1.

Programmes of Study for Design and Technology Capability

A general statement at each Key Stage and additional statements at each level.

Each programme of study has four sub-headings
* developing and using artefacts, systems and environments;
* working with materials;
* developing and communicating ideas;
* satisfying human needs and addressing opportunities.

General Requirements of the Programmes of Study

Pupils should work in a range of materials including:

Food; Textiles; Construction materials; Graphic media.

Design and technology activities should be set in a range of contexts including:

Home; School; Community; Recreation; Business and Industry

PROFILE COMPONENTS

The programmes of study described in the National Curriculum order for technology are intended to develop children's 'capability' in:

- design and technology;
- information technology.

These form the two profile components of technology.

Technology is a subject concerned with practical action. The emphasis throughout the technology order is on developing capability by engaging children in practical activities during which they must use and develop the resources of knowledge and skills from other areas of the curriculum in order to complete a course of action.

Information technology capability, the second of the two profile components, is developed through the application of information technology (IT) in all areas of the curriculum. We are only concerned with information technology within design and technology activities in this book.

DESIGN AND TECHNOLOGY CAPABILITY

This profile component specifies four attainment targets (ATs) which describe the process people go through when involved in design and technology activities. There are statements of attainment for each AT at ten levels; the first five levels cover Key Stages 1 and 2. The attainment targets are as follows:

- AT1 identifying needs and opportunities;
- AT2 generating a design;
- AT3 planning and making;
- AT4 evaluating.

ATTAINMENT TARGETS

▶ Identifying Needs and Opportunities (AT1)

This is the stage where discussion is concerned with identifying the opportunities for design and technology activities within the context of their work.

The National Curriculum requires all design and technology activities to be set in a range of contexts which should include: home; school; recreation; community; business and industry, reflecting the role of technology in our society. The context is the "...situation or set of circumstances in which the work is set". It is within these contexts that needs and opportunities should be identified.

▶ Context

Context is not the same as topic in which a central theme is examined through several different curriculum areas. For example, in a topic based on a visit to 'the supermarket', children might study the organisation of the shop, the pricing and range of products, the source of the products, the packaging, the replacement of the 'corner shop' by the supermarket, and many historical, geographical, mathematical and other aspects of the topic.

Design and technology work in such a topic might focus on any one (or more) of the listed contexts. For example, in the context of business and industry, children might create a shop environment within their classroom. This could be a focus for further activities which might include: security systems using electrical circuits; display and packaging of goods they have made; working models of machinery within the store such as conveyors, fork lifts and trucks.

The list of contexts in the order is not exclusive and may be extended to include other stimulating contexts such as 'story', providing opportunities for modelling characters or events, in the same way that they might paint a picture or write about the story. The intention of stating the range of contexts is to provide a balance in children's experiences.

Initially, the need or opportunity identified is likely to be one based on their own personal interests rather than one which relates to the needs of another person. Part of the progression within design and technology is the broadening of the child's awareness of other people's needs.

Sometimes, in order to control the breadth of experience and progression in learning, as well as for classroom management reasons, the teacher might wish to limit the children's choices, for example, in respect of the materials to be used. Setting constraints is quite acceptable, provided they allow the children to develop and use their own ideas. Explicit instructions provided by the teacher may allow the children to develop skills in making, but will not contribute to Attainment Target 1.

As the children grow in experience and capability, their freedom to decide within this attainment target can extend so that eventually (much later, in the secondary phase) they will be able to decide on the context itself, based on their own interests and observations.

It must be stressed that Attainment Target 1 does not release the teacher from the responsibility of deciding what the children should be doing. The teacher must set the boundaries within which the children are allowed to make decisions. For example, the teacher might use a particular project, e.g. making a moving character from a story, to develop the children's understanding of using levers and linkages to transmit motion. Some specific skills and knowledge will need to be taught so that the children can make decisions about using these systems to achieve the movement they choose on their character.

▶ Artefacts Systems and Environments

The programmes of study specify the sorts of things the children should make. It says that they should design and make:

- artefacts;
- systems;
- environments.

To most of us this is an unfamiliar way of categorising the outcomes of design and technology. We tend to think mainly of technology producing machines and other useful devices, i.e. artefacts. The inclusion of systems and environments certainly widens the range of possible outcomes.

Artefacts

An artefact is anything made by people. This includes items as diverse as a loaf of bread, a computer, a space satellite or a garment, and refers to useful as well as decorative and expressive items, such as a collage, a sculpture and other pieces of art. For the purpose of meeting the National Curriculum requirements, it is important to distinguish between those artefacts which are products of art and design, such as sculptures, and those of design and technology, such as machines.

Although at the moment there is no consensus on this, generally we consider the outcomes of design and technology activities to be those which are predominantly functional rather than predominantly aesthetic. This is not to deny that the aesthetic aspect is not also functional; things have to look good too. There is no definite boundary between these two categories and sometimes it is a matter of individual judgement.

Systems

A system is something made up of two or more parts used together to perform a function. It is difficult to think of any artefact that isn't used in conjunction with another, thereby forming a system (e.g. needle and thread or wheel and axle). Many artefacts are themselves made up of two or more parts and so form a system.

Systems can be organisational as well as concrete, for example, the school timetable. This is a human system, not a technological one.

To make a system, you might use pre-existing parts and rearrange them for some new, improved or different use, for example, using a construction kit such as Lego to build various models; building an electrical circuit from a selection of components; or making a cake from ingredients. We use systems all the time but seldom think of them that way. Needle and thread make up a system, though we don't refer to it as a 'button fixing system'.

Tracing these systems and seeing how they inter-relate can be interesting but the point of including systems in the programmes of study is that it allows designing and making to be done without the need, always, to be creating new artefacts from raw materials. Organisational systems within the classroom can provide useful opportunities for the children to manage their own environment.

Environments

Creating an environment to suit ourselves by altering the natural one is an activity not confined to Western technological society. In the developed Western world we have been so effective at this that it is almost impossible now to find any 'natural' environment at all. Many of our children are already sensitive to environmental issues and experiences in school should reflect this interest.

On a smaller scale, designing and making of environments is taking place already in many school classrooms. Often, the activity takes the form of rearranging, adding to and subtracting from some existing environment to improve it or to meet new needs. Examples include the 'home corner' or making part of the school grounds into a wildlife sanctuary. Artefacts might be designed and made if appropriate (e.g. bird-feeders in the garden) and systems might be developed (e.g. new ways of storing classroom resources) or the environment may be improved simply through rearranging what is already there.

▶ Generating a Design (AT2)

This is the stage which focuses on the ways in which the intended aim can be met. Much will depend on available resources of materials and processes, and the child's previous experience. This is an opportunity for the teacher to influence progression and breadth, leading the children into new areas of knowledge and skills. Evaluation (AT4) takes place throughout this phase when ideas are evaluated and accepted, modified or rejected.

The communication of the children's ideas is a vital component of this attainment target and may take a range of forms. As children's experience develops these will progress from verbal descriptions, illustrated by handling the materials to be used, in an approximation of their design; to producing simple annotated 2-D drawings; to more detailed drawings of particular parts of the design.

▶ Planning and Making (AT3)

This is the stage when the artefact, system or environment is created after having decided the specifications. Planning may include verbal descriptions of how work is to be tackled or divided amongst group members.

During this stage children will usually find that their first ideas need revising or even replacing in the light of experience as unpredicted problems arise. Discussion and re-design will occur, taking the children through activities associated with Attainment Targets 4 and 2. The process of refining the design may continue throughout the making stage.

The making part of the activity is the focus of design and technology. Children find this practical activity tremendously motivating, and children from a wide range of abilities achieve success. The concrete outcomes provide real feedback on the quality of the idea, i.e. does it do what you meant it to do?

A great deal of the success or failure of a design rests on the quality of the making. Inaccurate and careless construction may prevent a good idea from operating successfully.

▶ Evaluating (AT4)

The contribution of this attainment target to the process of design and technology occurs in two main ways:

1. Evaluation is continuous throughout a design and technology project from the time when, within a context, ideas are considered and accepted or rejected, through the process of organising and carrying out the practical activity, until the work is completed and the stage is reached of asking does it work, and if not, why not?

Throughout the progress of a project, as children evaluate their own work and teachers raise pertinent questions, the attainment targets may be visited again and again in a spiral pattern until the project is completed and a final evaluation is made.

Evaluations may be made on many levels. They may be simple questions, easily tested and answered, but sometimes things have to work on many levels. Does it operate well? Does it look pleasing? Is it non-polluting and safe to operate? The answers found may lead back to any of the other attainment target activities.

2. Evaluating systems and artefacts produced by other people may be the starting point for activity, for example examining pop-up greeting cards to stimulate ideas. This may provide opportunities, especially for older pupils, to evaluate technological products on a broader scale, asking questions about the moral issues that the creation, use and disposal of some products raise. (For example: the widespread use of disposable drinks containers; the use of lead-free petrol; or the use of long-lasting foam plastic hamburger boxes.) Evaluation of almost any product can lead to such issues.

Sometimes, time and other restraints will prevent the children from building things and their work will take the form of discussions, ideas and drawings. Although this is an important part of design and technology, it is really in making things that learning takes place most effectively and it is certainly the most rewarding part for the children. Design and technology is concerned above all with making things for some particular use.

Because this is a continuous, cyclic process (i.e. not just linear 1 to 2 to 3 to 4) it is not really possible or desirable to provide children with tasks intended to achieve any one attainment target alone. Instead, almost any design and technology activity will contribute, at different times, to each of the attainment targets, although some activities may concentrate more on one attainment target than another.

When children are doing design and technology, it may not be possible to tell by observation which attainment target best describes their activity at any given moment. The stages described by the attainment targets are not always separate. For example, realising that something isn't working as intended (AT4) and considering ways of improving it (AT2) often happen virtually together. You may find that you cannot distinguish easily between when children are planning, making or evaluating.

Although the attainment targets are numbered 1 to 4 it is not necessary for every activity to begin with Attainment Target 1. In fact, Attainment Target 4 can often provide a good starting point. For example, if children are to design and make a greeting card which incorporates a movement, it would be appropriate for them to begin by analysing and evaluating existing examples of this type of product. This would provide valuable and necessary experience for them to draw on during the design of their own card.

PROGRAMMES OF STUDY

The programmes of study define the nature of the activities through which the children will develop design and technology capability.

They require that children should design and make artefacts, systems and environments, and use a range of media to achieve their outcomes. These may include textiles, graphic media, construction materials and food.

The statements of what children should be taught are arranged under four headings:

- developing and using artefacts, systems and environments;
- working with materials;
- developing and communicating ideas;
- satisfying needs and addressing opportunities.

For each of these categories, there is a general statement at each key stage plus additional statements for each level. Teachers will find that many of these statements relate to activities which are already going on in the classroom. This is a reassuring aspect of the order and it is worth doing an audit of one's own teaching to see how much of current practice is relevant to these programmes of study. However, to meet the requirements of the National Curriculum, these experiences must be brought together and developed within the context of design and technology activities.

The non-statutory guidance suggests ways in which the programmes of study can be reorganised to aid the delivery and the development of progression. For example, you could identify the statements which relate to a specific area of knowledge or skills (referred to as strands) thus highlighting the progression, or you could group items together to provide a complete activity.

In the activity of joining materials, for example, pupils should be taught to:

- join materials and components in simple ways;
- use alternative ways of joining materials;
- combine materials to create others with enhanced properties;
- select and use appropriate methods of assembling a range of materials;
- join materials in permanent and semi-permanent forms.
  (Non-statutory guidance, page C7)

This strand identifies the elements in the programmes of study which are concerned with joining materials. Similar strands can be identified relating to the use of tools, energy, mechanisms, structures and others.

For most primary teachers who are attempting to coordinate the requirements of all the National Curriculum subjects within an integrated topic approach, an appropriate way of dealing with the programmes of study might be to engage the children in design and technology activities relating to their normal topic work, then to analyse the experience to see which elements of the programmes of study have been covered. Over the longer term, adjustments may be made to the children's activities to ensure that all of the requirements are met.

EQUAL OPPORTUNITIES

All children are required to engage in design and technology activities using the range of materials which include food and fabrics as well as construction materials and graphic media. This requirement will help to overcome some of the restrictive traditional views about which aspects of technology are appropriate for boys and which for girls.

Teachers, however, do need to be aware that there may be differences in the experiences that girls and boys have in their home environment, through the media and within their peer groups. These differences may affect their attitude to technology activities. Boys, for example, are more likely to have had experience with constructional toys or used tools and resistant materials to make things whilst girls are more likely to have been involved in role play and other traditional female activities. These differences may also be associated with certain social groups and cultures.

Apparent differences do not necessarily mean that girls have not developed a wide range of technological skills and understanding. By choosing contexts which are 'girl-friendly', they may feel more confident to engage in design and technology, at the same time broadening their experience, and thus avoiding the situation where they are involved only in technological tasks arising from women's traditional roles. Contexts should not be chosen which do not provide opportunities which appeal to *both* boys and girls. There is no part of school technology that is inappropriate for girls, and it is no less important for girls to be as capable as boys in making technological decisions and acting upon them.

If you are a woman, your role in technology education is doubly important. In addition to your teaching, you will provide a role model for the girls in your class. It is essential that girls feel they can have an equal role and equal choices in a technological society in which men have predominated in science and technology activities both in teaching and in industry.

There is some evidence to suggest that girls do better in single-sexed groups and teachers might consider whether children should work in mixed groups or whether there should be single-sexed groups. Whatever the form of organisation, the teacher must ensure that no child, boy or girl, simply adopts a passive role, either through reticence or being shouldered aside in the practical activities.

SPECIAL NEEDS

The breadth of design and technology allows access to a wide range of pupils with special needs, both very able children and those with learning difficulties. Two main

areas where special needs pupils may encounter difficulty are:
- communication; and
- making things.

There are many ways in which children can communicate their ideas and, whilst all children should experience the range, some may be more appropriate for special needs pupils than others. Children's confidence and ability in design and technology should not be undermined by their failure to master a specific skill. Collaborative writing, or the use of a tape recorder may allow difficulties with writing to be overcome, as would a photographic record or pictorial representation of the progress of a project.

Children who are handicapped in their muscular control and coordination may have difficulty with or be unable to use some tools and processes, and teachers may need to adapt work appropriately. There are usually several alternative ways of achieving a given technological outcome and team work permits children to undertake tasks suited to their abilities. Sensitive grouping can encourage children to share their expertise, and deficiencies in specific areas can be minimised.

ENVIRONMENTAL ISSUES

While developing awareness of materials and their properties, and learning to use them, children should be developing awareness of the social issues relating to these materials. The rapid depletion of the world's resources and the pressing problems of disposal and by-products are inseparable from consideration of the materials themselves. The very qualities that make materials so useful (e.g. resistance to biodegradation of most plastics) often create the most intractable difficulties (e.g. longevity of plastics litter). The recycling of materials is a good example of changing public awareness and one which young children can understand and practise.

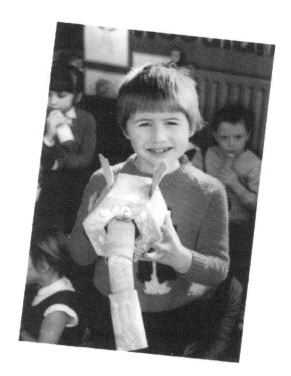

SUGGESTED READING

Technology in The National Curriculum. HMSO. 1990

The Curriculum from five to Sixteen. Curriculum Method 2. HMSO 1985

Design and Technology 5-12. Pat Williams and David Jinks.The Falmer Press. 1985

Design and Technology in Primary School Classrooms. Les Tickle. The Falmer Press. 1990

Design and Technology: Children's Engineering. Susan Dunn and Rob Larson. The Falmer Press. 1990

Teaching Craft Design and Technology. Peter Williams. Croom Helm. 1985

Primary School Technology. Peter Evans. TICST, Nottingham Polytechnic.

PART TWO

MANAGING DESIGN AND TECHNOLOGY

THE WORKSPACE

For most design and technology activities in the primary school, specialist facilities are not necessary. Some schools do have specialist rooms for which classes are timetabled. This means that a whole class will be engaged in practical activities at the same time which can be difficult to manage. There is no reason why this work should not proceed in the classroom using the normal facilities, and there are real advantages to be gained from this.

ORGANISING THE PUPILS

▶ Group Work

Many teachers have found it preferable to allow only a small group of children to work at their 'design and make' project at any one time whilst the remainder of the class are involved in other work. As the work proceeds, ideas and problems can be shared with the rest of the class so that the experience of one group of children benefits the rest. Not all children will have the same experiences; different groups will work on different aspects of a topic and experiences will be shared. As subsequent groups begin their project, they come to the activity with some potentially useful ideas gained from the activities of their classmates. They can build on this experience and not just repeat the previous work. Explaining, discussing and deciding details of a shared technological project rapidly enhances children's communication skills and their acquisition of an explicit technological vocabulary. Ideas come quickly, are evaluated and refined with others' experience to draw on.

The 'Blue Peter' approach where everyone does the same, to the teacher's explicit instructions, can be fun, but is not really design and technology because Attainment Targets 1, 2 and possibly 4 are not being addressed. Little thinking or decision making is being done,

except by the teacher. Design and technology always throws up unpredicted problems; if it does not, if all the difficulties have been forseen and avoided by the teacher, then the activity will be confined to craftwork, not design and technology. Problem solving is a necessary part of technology. Nevertheless, the Blue Peter approach may be useful on some occasions, particularly when the confidence of the teacher and the children needs developing, or when specific skills need to be taught.

The non-statutory guidance recommends teaching specific skills through a guided approach. Year 1 children may be introduced to a range of devices for joining materials, e.g. stapler, hole punch and paper fasteners, treasury tags, Blu-Tak, thread, etc. The children will need time to investigate and use the tools on a range of materials to gain the skill required for a specific task such as making a moving illustration of a nursery rhyme.

A moving nursery rhyme

During the period leading up to pancake day older children could make pancakes from a recipe. Discussions could then centre around the different fillings that can be served in pancakes, savoury and sweet, or toppings. The children then could design and cook their own recipe. This could lead on to an investigation of recipes of other countries where a pancake-like 'wrapper' is served with a filling, e.g. tortillas, pittas, chapatti and pasties. In this way the guided task allows the children to learn specific skills which will enable them to design.

▶ Time Allocation

We often find that teachers on design and technology courses become so absorbed by their activities that they miss breaks happily and work late! The same is true for children who often are highly motivated by such activities. It is worth capitalising on their enthusiasm by allowing them to work intensively on a project until its completion, achieving a balance with the other curriculum areas over the longer term. You will find that the richness of the learning experience and the broad overlap with other curriculum areas justifies the length of time taken by the task.

Aim for every child to be involved in a design and technology project at least once each term, perhaps only one table group at a time if the activity is an extended project. Don't start with all the class working at once - the demands on tools, equipment, materials and on you will be unmeetable.

▶ Planning the Task

The amount of planning which goes on before making begins, depends a great deal on the amount of experience the children have had. Very young children working with recycled material will often plan as they handle the boxes, ideas being stimulated by the shapes of the materials. Sometimes, the decision of what it is, is made at the end of the activity!

As their experience grows and skills develop, the materials and tools will be used in a more refined way and children will be more able to work to their own pre-determined plan.

When working with construction materials, some teachers encourage their pupils to draw possible solutions before they are tried out using real materials. Children may find this difficult and frustrating if their drawing skills are limited and they do not have enough technological experience to draw on. The only way for them to gain this experience is to work with the materials. Your children can explain their ideas to you or to each other before they begin to build, and their explanations will often need illustrating for clarity; this is the time for them to draw. This is how many craftsmen actually work, drawing only those parts of a design that need closer examination.

Try to find the time to sit with each group of children to talk through their plans and intended course of action before they begin. You may find that the children have more difficulty planning how they are going to carry out their work than they do planning what they are going to make.

▶ Avoiding Failure

In design and technology, as in any problem-solving situation, there will be times when children will encounter difficulties, and sometimes failure. This is not necessarily a bad thing unless they are completely demotivated by the experience. This should be avoided by encouraging them toward better solutions, sometimes by taking the opportunity to introduce new materials, teach a new skill, or by asking some pertinent questions. There can be no hard and fast rules about when the teacher should intervene to avoid disasters, despondency or blind alleys; this will be a matter of professional judgement.

▶ Aesthetics

Useful artefacts and environments, if they are going to be seen and used by people, should, if possible, be aesthetically pleasing. Contrary to much of the evidence around us, there is usually no reason why useful things cannot also be beautiful, or at least not ugly, and this is true of children's models, too.

All primary teachers encourage their children to present their work neatly and attractively, and it is important that this tradition is applied to work in design and technology. Care and accuracy in working techniques are more likely to produce quality work which performs well and of which the child can be proud. Shoddy working techniques usually lead to frustration and failure.

Paints, clay, fabrics and yarns, papier mâché and the range of art and craft materials commonly found in the classroom all have a contribution to make to design and technology activities. Considerations of proportion, colour, texture and finish must form a part of the design process through which the children work.

▶ Recording for Breadth and Progression

Recording the children's work to control depth, breadth and progression imposes a considerable work load on teachers. Whatever recording system is used, it must be simple enough to be manageable across a whole class yet detailed enough to provide useful information for the teacher and colleagues. Eventually, there may be a standardised format for National Curriculum records but meanwhile, schools will have to develop their own recording schedules.

As the statutory requirement is based on the levels of attainment as defined in the order for technology, some system of recording an individual's achievement through these levels must be kept. This is a legal requirement. However, the statements of attainment are so very general that they do not give sufficient information to inform teachers about what the children have actually done. Control of the progression and balance of the children's learning will demand an additional, more detailed level of recording.

Design and technology is not primarily concerned with the acquisition of knowledge for its own sake but with the ability to use effectively the processes described by the attainment targets to identify and solve practical problems. Consequently, progression resides in the subtlety of the decisions the children have to make for themselves and the appropriateness of the solutions they find, as well as in the quality of their workmanship. Balance is found in the range of materials and processes

they use and the contexts in which their work is set; these should start close to the child's own experience and extend out into the world of other people.

Records need to provide the following information:

- statements of attainment in each of the four attainment targets for each child;
- topics followed by the class; design and technology activities developed within each topic; and the aspects of the programmes of study covered. This record could be maintained by the children themselves as they complete each task;
- knowledge and skills the children are developing through their design and technology activities. (See Appendix 5 for some suggested systems for recording this information.)

ORGANISING THE RESOURCES

A requirement of the programmes of study is that children should use a range of materials which includes:
- food;
- textiles;
- construction materials;
- graphic media.

Schools may already have a good range of resources for art and for working with textiles and food as there has been a long tradition of these types of activity in primary schools. However, it may take several years before every school has the broad range of resources to work equally well in all four of these groups of materials.

It is important to begin design and technology activities with the resources you have and with which you are familiar, increasing the range as the need arises and confidence grows. There are many valuable activities children can undertake with the very simple tools and materials you have already: scissors; glue; tape; paper fasteners.

Below we discuss the range of resources you might consider, and organisational issues with which you will need to deal.

▶ Working with Food

The range of equipment needed to work with food is, perhaps, best stored together to form a school kit. Some schools will already have a dedicated area for food preparation where all the necessary resources are kept; this might be a spare classroom, part of a shared craft area or an area in the staff room. Sometimes the equipment is stored on mobile trolleys and trundled into classrooms as it is required.

Whichever system your school adopts, it is important to keep in mind the stringent hygiene precautions that must be applied always when food is being prepared. Ideally, the area where you work should only be used for preparing food. The potential dangers of using the same work surface for painting, claywork and sawing wood or plastics as well as for preparing food are obvious, and though it may not be realistic to allocate an area of your classroom only for food preparation, perhaps this could be done somewhere else in the school.

Cookers

Some facility for cooking food is essential otherwise the range of the children's activities will be very restricted. There are several main options to consider.

An electric ring which plugs into the mains, can provide a useful heat source. It limits you to one-ring cooking but has the advantage of mobility.

A small, mobile cooker, such as a Baby Belling, can be fitted onto a trolley and moved from class to class and plugged in as required. The small oven, grill and two rings considerably extends the range of things that can be made.

A microwave oven is fast and consumes less energy than the conventional cooker, although it isn't quite so versatile. Those that also have a grill offer extended possibilities.

A conventional cooker provides the resource with which the children will be most familiar. This must, of course, be installed by a qualified person and will need to be located in a dedicated area.

Cooking Equipment

The range of cooking equipment you provide, i.e. saucepans, baking tins, mixing bowls, dishes and other utensils, will depend on the cooking facility. Whatever you choose, it is wise to select the best quality, particularly in the case of saucepans and baking tins, which often last longer and are easier to keep clean. Unbreakable dishes should be used whenever possible, and any glassware should be able to withstand sudden extremes of temperature as when a hot liquid is poured into it. Pyrex is of this type.

Equipment sold through the reputable educational suppliers will have been chosen with safety as well as quality in mind and it is worth following their recommendations.

Handling Tools

Some of the most useful kitchen tools have sharp blades, e.g. knives, graters and peelers. They pose a safety problem, not only during their use but also when washing up. Small children may not have adequate wrist control to manage these tools safely and often assistance will be required when these tools are used.

A good food processor, perhaps for the teachers' use only, can ease these problems. Children making toppings for pizza-toast or sandwiches for example, could be provided with the range of ready sliced or chopped ingredients from which to choose.

Hygiene

It is worth giving the children some notice when they have to prepare food. Not all children come to school neatly scrubbed and in clean clothes, and this may be a chance to influence their standards of personal hygiene, if necessary. Decide with the children on the standards you wish to exact, e.g. special care in washing, perhaps a bath, long hair tied back, an apron or smock, etc. They could help to produce the guidelines; the school cooks might provide them with some useful advice.

All the equipment used for food preparation will need to be washed after use. Facilities will need to be made available for this and for clean and regularly laundered cloths and tea-towels.

Food Rotation

Many teachers provide the necessary food for their activities on the day it is required and this ensures that it is fresh. If there is a store cupboard in school where basic items are kept, make sure packets and tins are dated, and old produce thrown away. Dry foods like flour and sugar could be kept in plastic containers with sealed lids to avoid possible contamination or infestation. A small fridge-freezer would be useful both for storage and food preparation.

▶ Working with Textiles

The fabrics available in school will probably include cotton, felts and hessian. This range can be extended very cheaply by recycling cleaned, discarded clothes to include wool, knitted fibres, waterproof fabric and fabrics with other properties. Examining the way that garments are put together can provide the children with some useful insights into their manufacture.

Parents can also help by sending in left-over balls of wool or remnants of material from their own use.

Trays with small containers, such as margarine cartons, will provide useful storage for threads, beads, sequins, buttons and other fasteners, and the numerous other small components which gradually can be collected together. Pins are best provided stored on a pin cushion.

Certain resources probably will be centrally stored and shared. A sewing machine should form part of this resource and an iron and ironing board or length of table-felt for ironing upon. The use of the iron might, for safety reasons, be reserved for adults.

Plastic boxes, which stack neatly and are light-weight, could be used to store other equipment needed for working with textiles. They might include fabric printing equipment and dyes, a wider range of threads than those stored in the classroom, sewing hoops, cards and frames for weaving, knitting needles, etc. Many of these items will be used for work in art as well as design and technology.

▶ Graphic Media

This is an area for which schools will already be well resourced. Each class or shared area should have its own range of art media easily accessible to the children. These resources will support work in all areas of the curriculum as children illustrate written work and communicate their ideas in a graphical form.

Specialist equipment such as marbling kits, print-making materials and spray diffusers, may form part of a general school resource along with fabric crayons and paints and those resources which are not in daily use.

Good quality art materials need careful management to avoid waste and spoilage. Paint brushes may be ruined if they are not washed and stored properly as will drawing pens (if left resting on their tips).

Felt pens need storing in a way that makes it easy to notice when tops have been left off. Encouraging the children to take the responsibility for looking after these resources is an important aspect of classroom management.

▶ Working with Construction Materials

It is important that you and the children begin with the tools and materials with which you are familiar, introducing new ones only when you feel the need for them. The equipment you have now in your classroom will enable your children to become involved in design and technology.

Few tools are designed specifically for children's use and most adult tools are unsuited to the size of children's hands. This considerably restricts the range of tools you can provide for your class. Most teachers prefer to have a group of not more than six or eight children working on technological activities at any one time, and this reduces further the numbers of tools needed in the classroom. (See Appendix 1 for guidance on selecting tools.)

Increasingly, educational suppliers are providing a comprehensive range of resources for design and technology activities. (See Appendix 3 for some useful addresses.)

There are several primary school tool kits available. These are usually sold complete with a storage system and often are described as class kits. They vary greatly in the choice of tools, and in the way they are stored, but if your school can afford to buy such a system, by 'shopping around' you will probably be able to purchase a kit which meets your needs.

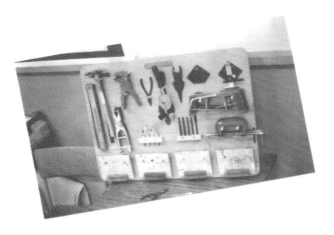

Trent International Centre for School Technology (TICST) tool kit

Your class kit must demand an absolute minimum of maintenance. For this reason, and more importantly for your children's safety, it should contain no 'edge' tools (tools with a knife-like blade) and then the kit can be made as freely accessible to the children as maths equipment or paints.

Create a system for storing your tools which is easy to manage. A shadow board system is ideal as you can see at a glance which tools are missing. Labelled drawers or boxes might be an alternative but remember that because the contents are not immediately visible, things can go missing unnoticed.

Ideally, each class should have its own basic resources of tools and consumables, growing in range with the experience of the teacher and the children. The younger the children, the more restricted will be the range of tools offered to them. Scissors, a stapler and a hole punch, together with adhesives and fasteners of various types could be enough for Year 1 children to use for constructions with paper, card and boxes.

If resources have to be shared, then design and technology activities have to be timetabled. This means less flexibility for work to be on-going and to respond to children's enthusiasm. Another problem with shared resources is maintaining and keeping track of them. Booking-out systems might have to be developed.

Some tools are not needed often enough to justify having them in each classroom. Make up a 'school kit' for more specialised tools such as a drill and drill-stand, and soldering irons.

▶ Consumable Resources

As your experience and confidence grows, you will find yourself acquiring a widening range of resources suitable for design and technology. Keeping them under control will be important if they are to remain accessible to the children without taking over your classroom. (See Part 4:1 for further guidance on selecting resources.)

The cost of resourcing technological activities always worries teachers, especially the continuing costs of consumable materials needed to support such activities across the curriculum. Both you and your children have to be sensitive to the price of the materials you use. Wherever appropriate, use recycled materials to keep the costs down.

▶ Recycled Materials

Recycled materials

These materials can provide a valuable resource for technology with the added bonus of providing an opportunity to develop some of the ideas set out in the National Curriculum order for science and maths.

Establish some categories of materials and encourage the children to sort the materials they bring into school, identifying the similarities and differences between materials so that they can be classified. The materials may be sorted either according to type, e.g. card, plastic, fabrics, wood, drinks cans, other metals, or according to shape, e.g. cuboids of different sizes, cylindrical objects.

The children's ability to discriminate may be developed through these sorting activities. Encourage the children to sort according to more than one criterion, e.g. boxes smaller than a given measure, or cans made of aluminium (you can use a magnet to separate the steel from the aluminium which you can trade in for its scrap value).

Select interesting-looking boxes from those that the children bring in and produce a 'shape' table. Packaging in shops is becoming very elaborate and it is possible to purchase goods packaged in cubes, cylinders, triangular, hexagonal and octagonal prisms without having to search too far. Looking at packaging provides a good starting point for work on solid shapes and encourages the children to look out for interesting shapes from their own surroundings.

Lengths of wood and dowel may be stored in simple 'home-made' systems, as can wooden wheels.

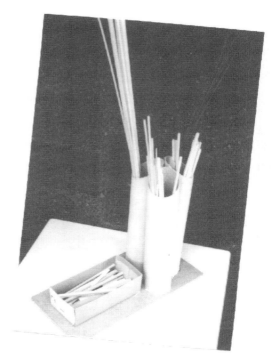

Storage for lengths of wood and dowel

Storage for wheels

▶ Small Components

A wide range of items falls into the 'small component' category and includes many of the stationery items you probably have in the classroom already, e.g. Blu-Tak, paper fasteners, drawing pins, etc. (Throughout Part 4 reference will be made to many small components and some of their uses.) Make as wide a range as possible of these items accessible to the children. A good system is to store small components in plastic containers in a tray. For a list of the items we regularly use, see Appendix 2.

▶ Storage for small components

Whichever system you employ for storing materials, tools and components, try to minimise the amount of work it creates for you by choosing storage systems which the children can maintain easily and you can check easily. Resources hidden away are more likely to become untidy than those which are a visible part of your classroom environment.

▶ Recycling Children's Models

When the children's models contain expensive parts, especially electrics and timber, it may be appropriate to recycle these components for future use. After work has been displayed in school, the children will probably want to take it home. Some schools operate a loan system where each child who contributed to the model can keep it for a specified period before passing it on. Eventually the model can be returned to school for recycling.

HEALTH AND SAFETY

Classrooms have always been very safe places for children to be in and there is no reason why design and technology activities should alter this.

It is important that children develop safe working habits and positive attitudes towards health and safety issues; design and technology activities provide a valuable opportunity for this. More effective than a list of prohibitions (or do's and don'ts) is to approach safety from two perspectives:

- safe environment; and
- safe practice.

▶ Safe Environment

The tools you decide to make available will depend on the age and experience of the children. Tools with sharp-edged blades should be avoided as well as any too large or heavy for the children to handle. Construction materials which need to be held in a large vice to be worked on are inappropriate for the children, for example, sawing large sections of wood, or bending thick metal.

If you permit electrical tools (e.g. hot-melt glue gun or soldering iron), you may be required by your local authority to use specific kinds of equipment (e.g. electrical safety cut-out devices, low voltage or cordless soldering irons, or heat-proof leads to prevent accidental damage from the tips of the soldering irons).

Some materials are less benign than they appear. For example, rigid plastic sheets (e.g. Perspex) give off an irritant dust if sandpapered. It is unsafe also to burn even small pieces of any plastic material.

Consider the safety aspecys of how your resources are stored. For example, it is safer to handle tools clipped to a board than piled in a box and sharp knives should not be freely accessible.

▶ Safe Practice

Everyday good housekeeping, such as putting tools and materials back after use, is a contribution that the children can learn to make quickly towards a safe working environment. It also can help to organise work patterns, by restricting the number of children around the tools at one time, or re-arranging tables to keep clear space around anyone using a glue gun or sewing machine, or by co-ordinating their work so that you can supervise particular activities together. Creating a safe working environment is one type of activity referred to in the programmes of study.

The safe use of tools is something that must be taught. For example, materials being worked, i.e. cut or drilled, should not be held in the hand. Make sure the children use a cutting board (sometimes called a bench hook) when sawing. When drilling, do not allow fingers close to the drill end although injury is unlikely with a hand drill. The working end of a tool is never a safe place; use a G-clamp or a clamping device fitted to a drill-stand.

The use of sharp cutting tools and heating tools such as glue guns and electric irons, in particular, require close supervision and the children must be shown correct methods of using these tools.

Many teachers prefer to have only one group of children working with tools and materials at a time. The children can understand readily the hazards of pushing, crowding around or snatching tools and learn to moderate their enthusiastic behaviour, perhaps devising rotas for using equipment.

Your local authority may have a code of practice for practical activities or some specific requirements, and your school should locate this information.

There may also be local guidance or requirements about what to do in case of accidents. Some authorities issue quite explicit instructions and it is obviously important to know what these are before they are needed. Further advice may be found in the suggested reading below.

SUGGESTED READING

Be Safe. Association for Science Education (ASE). College Lane, Hatfield, Herts AL10 9AA. Tel: 07072 67411.

PART THREE

OPPORTUNITIES FOR DESIGN AND TECHNOLOGY

STARTING POINTS

There are many ways in which design and technology can be introduced into the classroom, some providing an open-ended approach where children are able to identify the opportunities themselves, whilst others are much more constrained.

Both of these approaches are necessary. If you are introducing design and technology for the first time or if you are apprehensive about managing a very open-ended situation in an area of the curriculum which is new to you, then a more constrained approach may be best until you and your children gain confidence and experience. It will also make it easier for you to control breadth and balance through the introduction of new skills and knowledge.

▶ Topic

Most teachers who approach work through a topic or theme will be familiar with identifying opportunities in the main curriculum areas from this starting point. For example, you may plan your topics by producing a topic web showing the opportunities for mathematics, science, language, artwork, music, historical, environmental and other work.

Most topics have some potential for design and technology activities, and teachers will need to identify these opportunities as they plan the broader aspects of the topic. In this way, design and technology will become an integral part of normal curriculum planning, and learning in the other areas of the curriculum will support the activities in design and technology.

Don't be too concerned if all topics do not appear to have the same potential, as this will almost certainly be the case. Some topics will have a strong historical bias; others may be chosen specifically for the language opportunities (a story-based topic, perhaps). In your planning, try to create a balance in the topics

you choose, between those which are rich in opportunities for design and technology and those which are less so.

▶ National Curriculum Contexts

The order for technology requires that design and technology activities take place within a range of contexts including home, school, recreation, community, business and industry. There are two main ways of setting design and technology work in these contexts.

Contexts such as the home and school are popular topics in themselves and are as rich in design and technology as they are in other curriculum areas. For example, in the topic 'the home', children might build environments for mini-beasts, or model a house complete with working light circuits and curtains from fabric they have printed themselves.

Aspects of topics based on other starting points may be developed within the National Curriculum contexts. For example, a topic based on 'our town' could include a visit to a fast-food outlet. This might lead to the children making 'designer-burgers' with more interesting ingredients, or designing more environment-friendly packaging.

▶ Visits

Visits are excellent starting points for design and technology and for thematic work generally, providing the children with motivating, first-hand experience on which subsequent work can be based. Observation of technological artefacts and systems in their environment can help to provide the children with some necessary insights into how they work. These experiences can be developed and extended as the children become involved in their own, related tasks.

Observational drawings will focus the children's attention on particular functions and moving parts, and important ideas can be drawn out through discussion.

► Story

Listening to and reading stories is an important part of every child's school experience and there are many opportunities provided by stories to develop some design and technology activities.

Because stories are not always linked with a topic, they can sometimes provide the balance of opportunity if a chosen topic does not lend itself to design and technology or if the teacher wants to keep the focus of the topic in another area of the curriculum. An opportunity for design and technology arising in the story may be the starting point of a mini-topic, or a chance for a specific group of children to focus on design and technology as part of the rotation of groups engaging in practical activities.

Work based on *The Iron Man* by Ted Hughes might include models of machinery or of the 'iron man', complete with flashing red eyes. This same story could lead into science investigations of materials, particularly metals.

► Local Events

Events will occur which can be used as a starting point. There may be road works nearby which could be visited with a view to developing design and technology activities; building working models of some of the machinery, for example. A visit to a theatre or a visiting theatre group may provide some ideas from which might be developed some short activities, e.g. making puppets or moving 2-D faces.

► Challenges

The challenge approach can take many different forms and it is important to be clear about what the children are to learn.

1. When children are involved in open-ended tasks in which they make decisions about what is to be done and how (AT1), there are likely to be gaps in their experience which the teacher must redress through a more content-specific approach. For example, in a topic on air, or capitalising on the opportunity provided by a windy day, the children may be challenged to make a kite that flies. Here the teacher will have identified the opportunity (AT1) leaving the children to focus on the designing, making

and evaluating of their kite and to gain experience of using and controlling the energy of the wind.

To ensure a group of children have experience of using specific skills or knowledge in a practical activity, a focused task may be set. For example, use a motor to power a vehicle, or use Lego to make a slow-moving, level-crossing barrier. Here too, AT1 has been by-passed and the opportunity to generate a design proposal (AT2) has been constrained. The focus of this task is on ATs 3 and 4. The teacher has constrained the tasks so that, in the first example, the children will learn how to use a motor and in the second they will have had an opportunity to use gears.

2. Focusing on design and technology across a class, a year group or even the school is another approach. This is common in other areas of the curriculum where there might be a 'science week', a 'book week' or an 'art week', when usual activities are suspended and everyone's attention is focused on one area of the curriculum. A theme may be set which is then developed by each class. For example, in one school, the challenge was to make a musical instrument that played automatically. The headteacher's office was converted into a 'Patent Office' where designs and plans had to be registered. Other challenges might be to make things which fly, or make an animal that moves.

This approach may be in response to an LEA organised event such as a 'Science and Technology Fair' in which all schools can participate. This is an opportunity for the whole school to look at progression. By evaluating the outcomes of the activity, it is possible to begin to identify what might be expected from each year group in terms of skills, knowledge and process. This activity might precede a 'Professional Training Day' where these matters may be further discussed.

3. Many books give ideas for 'egg-races', i.e. short activities where a challenge is set and materials and time are constrained. Some of these can be fun but try to avoid challenges which are overly specific (e.g. make a vehicle travel five metres, drop a marble, etc.) as their solutions often demand higher levels of

precision than it is reasonable to expect of primary children and often they leave little room for imaginative responses. The girls, especially, can be put off by this.

GENERATING IDEAS

▶ Open -ended Situations

Attainment Target 1 requires children to identify their own opportunities for design and technology activities but this doesn't imply a situation where the children can learn anything they like. The teacher must consider the potential of the starting point so that the children's learning can be guided to ensure proper breadth and progression, both as defined by the National Curriculum and arising from the children's interests.

For example, taking a visit to a windmill as a starting point, there are two main ways in which ideas for activities may be identified:

- looking within the starting point for aspects which the children could explore. For example: sack-hoist; grain joggler; sieving/sorting; weighing machines; milling; bread making; sails and fantail; the tower; lightning conductor;

- looking broadly around the starting point to identify areas into which the work may expand. For example : weather / wind measuring, recording, experiencing, through kites; watermills; sails - on the mill, on boats, on land yachts; making bread.

When the stimulus or the starting point is motivating and rich in potential, the children will have their own ideas of what they might like to make. The teacher must be ready to accept their ideas if they are sensible and realistic. The potential must be considered in advance so that the teacher can guide the children to observe and ask questions about those aspects which are likely to provide a starting point for design and technology.

▶ Focused Tasks

Here, the teacher will have a clear idea of the specific skills and knowledge the children

will use during their activity. Even when the content of the activity is partly defined in this way, it is still possible for the children to be involved in all four attainment targets. For example, at Key Stage 1, the children might make a sandwich for an afternoon tea-party. They would be shown how to assemble a sandwich and then be provided with a range of fillings from which to choose.

Similarly, at Key Stage 2, the children might be required to model a character from a story and make a part of it move. They would be shown some mechanisms which create movement (e.g. lever systems) which they could incorporate into their design.

IDEAS FOR DESIGN AND TECHNOLOGY ACTIVITIES

The ideas illustrated on the following pages are set within popular primary school topics and provide a range of examples of design and technology activities. These are not intended as recipes but as indicators of the kinds of things children might make in their topic work. You will find that many of the ideas can be adapted and used in a much wider range of topics. For example, water rockets (in the section on *Castles*) might be made as part of a topic on flight, or space, or as a 'School Fair' fundraiser. Making bread might occur after a visit to a mill, or as part of a topic on farming, or on food.

The range of ideas illustrated for each topic is much broader than would normally be covered. You will need to guide your children towards those which extend the breadth and balance of their experience.

You may find it appropriate, when planning, to select ideas from more than one of the topics here. For example, a topic on *Homes* could extend to looking at the castle in its role as a home for its inhabitants; some of the castle ideas may then be appropriate for the homes topic.

▶ National Curriculum Contexts

The National Curriculum order for technology requires that design and technology activities be developed within a range of contexts including home, school, community, recreation, business and industry. (See Part 1, page 2.)

Within most topics, the children's activities can be focused toward one or more of these contexts as the teacher controls the breadth of the children's experience.

The following matrix indicates some of the links between the National Curriculum contexts and the topics that we have illustrated in this section.

▶ *The Matrix*

In the *Animals* topic, for example, opportunities exist for working within the context of the home, if the children's own pets are considered as the focus for design and technology work. Making homes for mini-beasts which are collected for studying as part of science work, is within the context of school. Creating an attractive garden environment for local wildlife may be seen as being within a community context.

As the topic progresses and the focus changes, different groups of children may be involved in activities based in different contexts, e.g. one group making a wildlife garden while another is making the 'enormous crocodile'

(from the book *The Enormous Crocodile* by Roald Dahl).

The range of contexts in which work may be set can be wider than those listed in the National Curriculum. Stories and literature, both traditional and modern, may provide a context for design and technology work in which several National Curriculum contexts are subsumed. For example, the story of *The Lighthouse Keeper's Lunch* can stimulate exciting design and technology work. The story can be seen as being in the home, the community, and business and industry contexts. Topics based on the environment, both local and global, may be particularly broad in their range of contexts, and children in the class may work in all of the National Curriculum contexts in just one topic.

In practice, few topics are restricted to any one context; the richer the topic is in design and technology learning opportunities, the more contexts it is likely to span.

The range of National Curriculum contexts must be covered throughout each Key Stage; perhaps within any one year some context may not be deeply covered. This should not matter so long as there is sufficient breadth of experience within the Key Stage.

◀———————— National Curriculum ————————▶

Topics	Contexts				
	Home	School	Community	Recreation	Business and Industry
Animals	Pets	Mini-beasts	Local wildlife	Bird watching Story	Farming
Castles	Life in a castle		Local history		
The coast			Lifeboats, lighthouses	Holidays	Fishing
Fairground and circus			Travelling people	Entertainment	Sideshows
Air	Observing weather Seed dispersal		Windmills	Kites	Transport
Homes	Facilities in the home		Local environment	Gardening	Building homes

◀———————— Themes within the topic ————————▶

Meeting the 'context' requirements of the National Curriculum Order for Technology

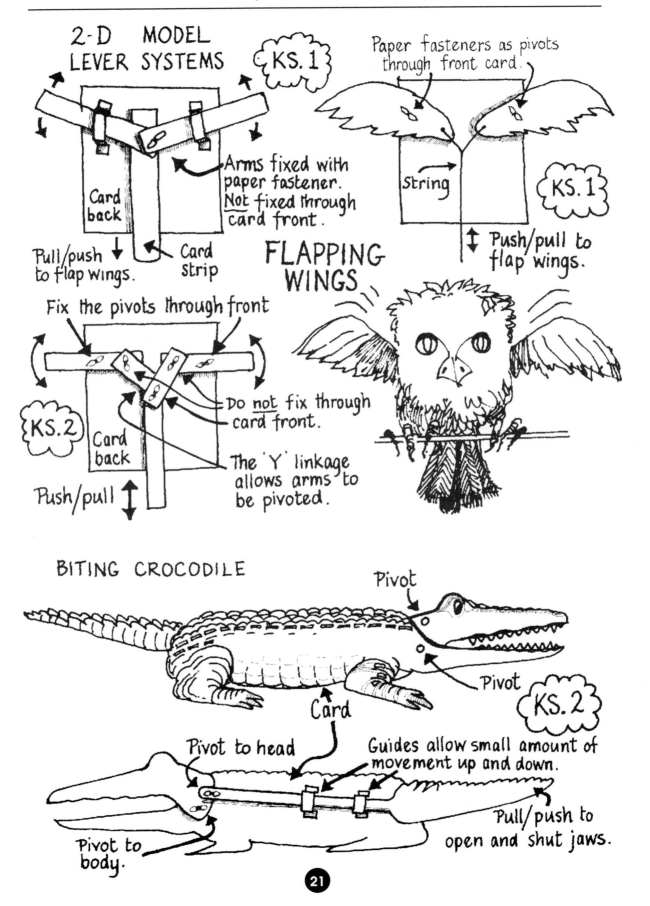

2-D MODEL LEVER SYSTEMS

KS.1

Card back

Pull/push to flap wings.

Card strip

Arms fixed with paper fastener. Not fixed through card front.

Paper fasteners as pivots through front card.

String

Push/pull to flap wings.

KS.1

FLAPPING WINGS

Fix the pivots through front

KS.2

Card back

Push/pull

Do not fix through card front.

The 'Y' linkage allows arms to be pivoted.

BITING CROCODILE

Pivot

Pivot

Card

KS.2

Pivot to head

Guides allow small amount of movement up and down.

Pull/push to open and shut jaws.

Pivot to body.

3·D MODEL : HINGES

KS.1/2

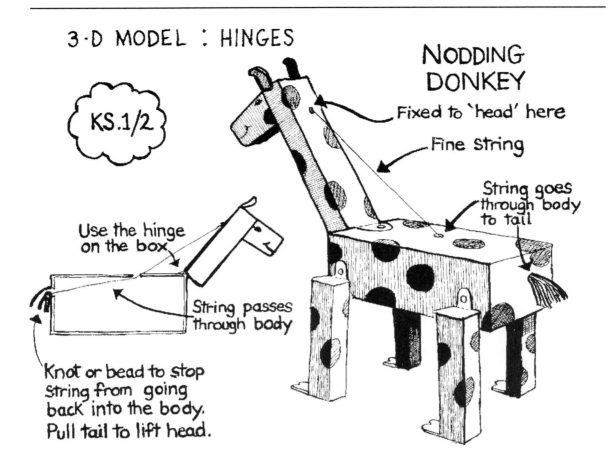

NODDING DONKEY

Fixed to 'head' here

Fine String

String goes through body to tail

Use the hinge on the box

String passes through body

Knot or bead to stop string from going back into the body. Pull tail to lift head.

Card links fixed with paper fasteners.

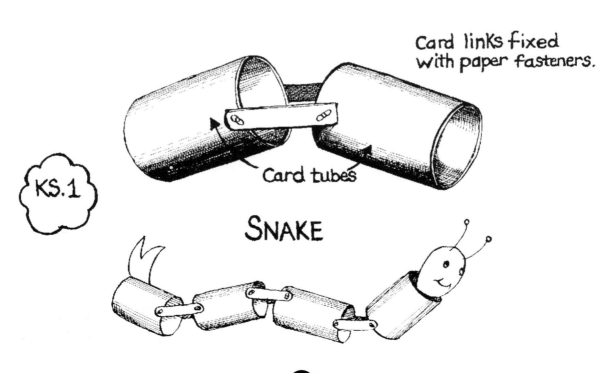

Card tubes

KS.1

SNAKE

3-D MODEL : ROTATION SYSTEMS

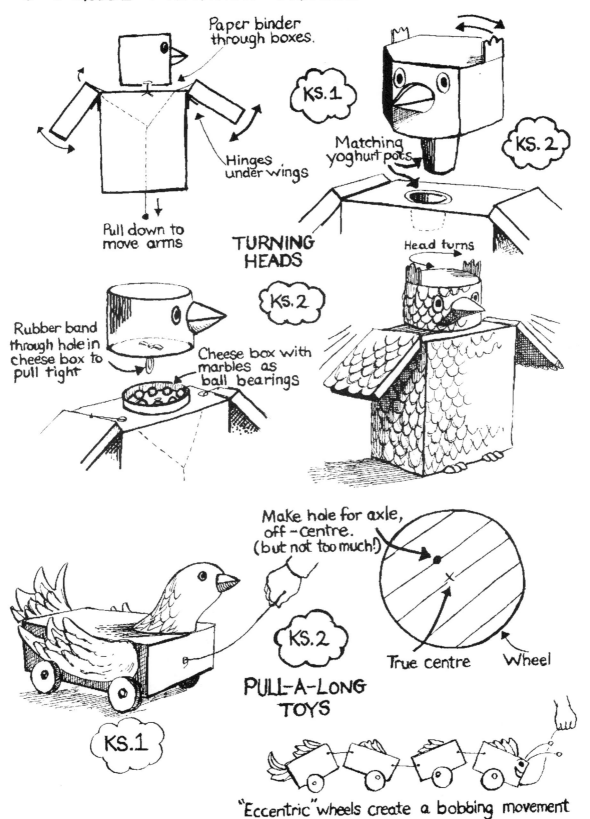

Paper binder through boxes.

KS.1

Pull down to move arms

Hinges under wings

KS.2

Matching yoghurt pots

Head turns

TURNING HEADS

KS.2

Rubber band through hole in cheese box to pull tight

Cheese box with marbles as ball bearings

Make hole for axle, off-centre. (but not too much!)

True centre   Wheel

KS.2

PULL-A-LONG TOYS

KS.1

"Eccentric" wheels create a bobbing movement

23

ENVIRONMENT : ENCOURAGING WILDLIFE

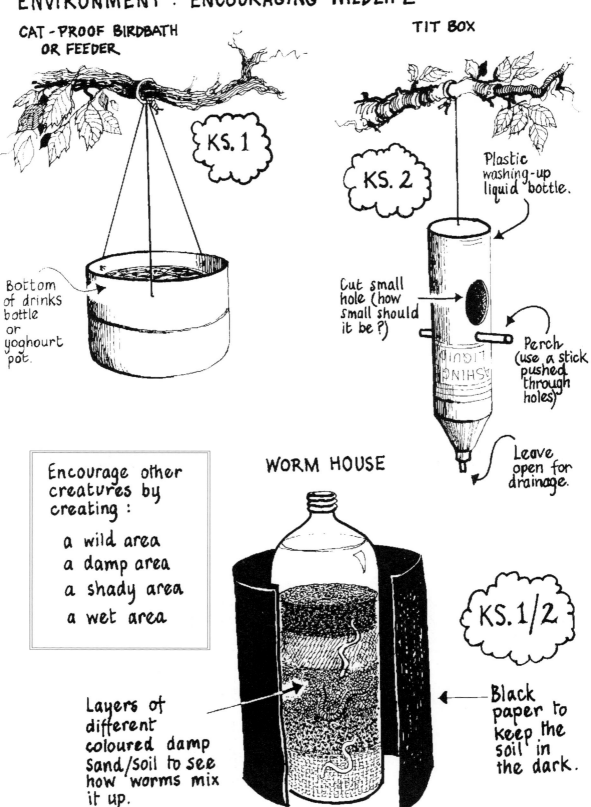

CAT-PROOF BIRDBATH OR FEEDER

KS.1

Bottom of drinks bottle or yoghourt pot.

TIT BOX

KS.2

Plastic washing-up liquid bottle.

Cut small hole (how small should it be?)

Perch (use a stick pushed through holes)

Leave open for drainage.

Encourage other creatures by creating:

a wild area
a damp area
a shady area
a wet area

WORM HOUSE

KS.1/2

Layers of different coloured damp sand/soil to see how worms mix it up.

Black paper to keep the soil in the dark.

ENVIRONMENT : ENCOURAGING WILDLIFE

MAKING WILD BIRD CAKE

Chopped-up bacon rind

MELTED LARD OR DRIPPING

WILD BIRD SEED

KS.1/2

Get an adult to do this.

Yoghourt pot (take care the hot lard doesn't melt the pot!)

YOGHOURT BLACK CHERRY

String to hang the bird cake when it is set hard.

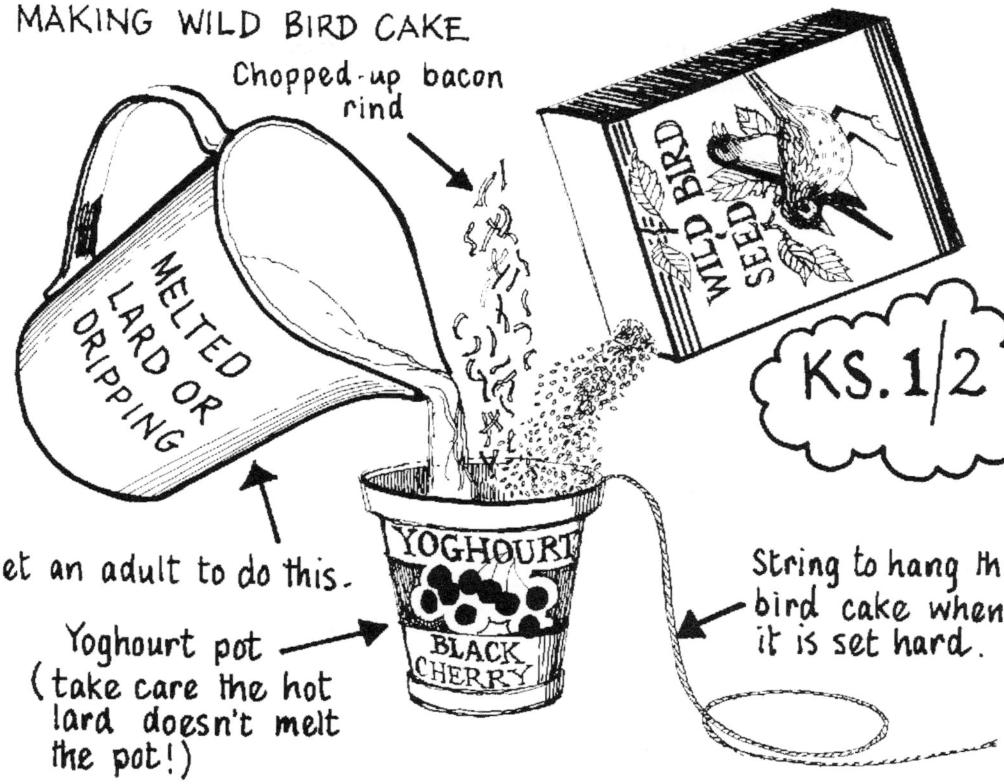

BUTTERFLY/MOTH BREEDING CAGE

KS 2

Use a staple gun.

Removable lid.

▷ Encourage butterflies into the school garden.

▷ Find out which plants to grow, eg. buddleia, nettles, etc.

▷ Collect eggs with the plant on which you find them and watch their development.

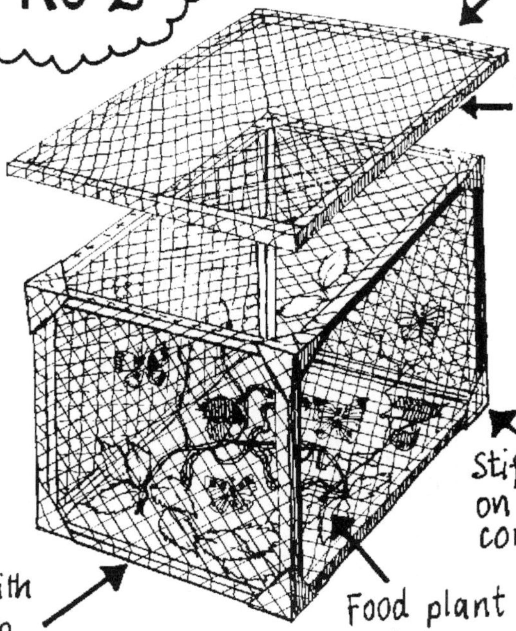

Stiffening on corners.

Space frame covered with fine mesh net stapled to frame.

Food plant and branches.

CASTLE KEEP

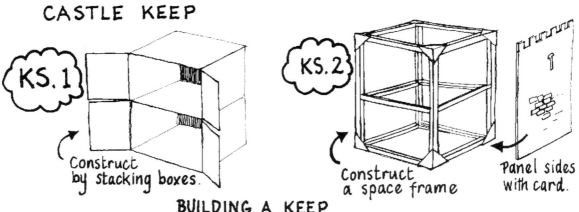

KS.1

Construct by stacking boxes.

KS.2

Construct a space frame

Panel sides with card.

BUILDING A KEEP

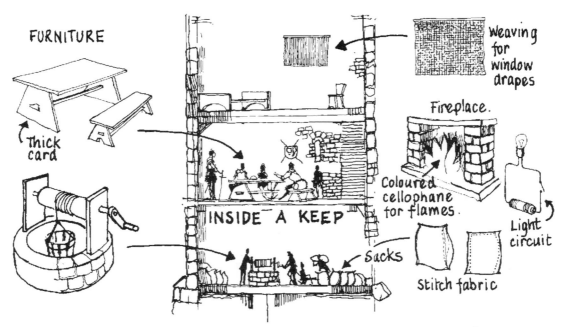

FURNITURE

Thick card

Weaving for window drapes

Fireplace.

Coloured cellophane for flames.

Light circuit

INSIDE A KEEP

Sacks

Stitch fabric

THE CASTLE WALLS

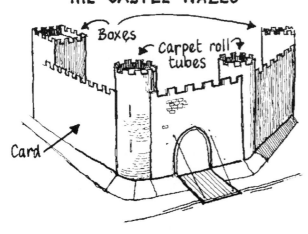

Boxes

Carpet roll tubes

Card

RAISING THE DRAWBRIDGE

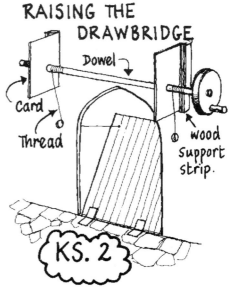

Dowel

Card

Thread

wood support strip.

KS.2

MEDIEVAL FEAST
MAKING BREAD
Basic recipe:
1½ lb (675g) flour.
1 packet dried yeast.
¾ pint (375ml) water.

Optional:
1 teaspoonful salt.
1 oz (28g) margarine.

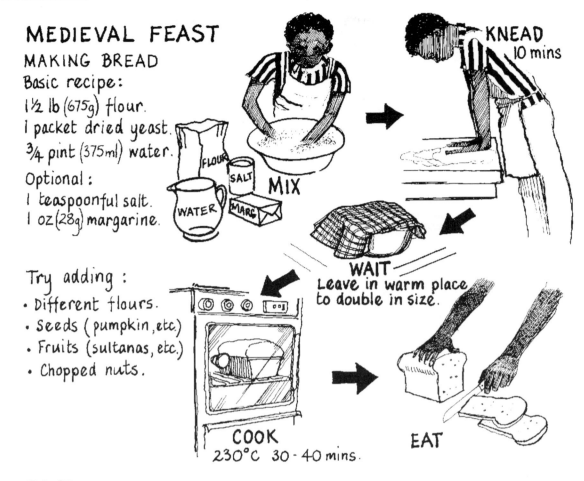

MIX

KNEAD
10 mins

WAIT
Leave in warm place to double in size.

COOK
230°C 30-40 mins.

EAT

Try adding:
- Different flours.
- Seeds (pumpkin, etc.)
- Fruits (sultanas, etc.)
- Chopped nuts.

RABBIT STEW

Rabbit joints
Vegetables
Stock cube

Which vegetables did medieval people have?

Which fruits?

MAKING GINGER BEER
Add to: 4½ Litres (gallons) of boiled and cooled water.

Ginger Beer Plant

From a home brew shop.

- Leave for 3/4 days.
- Siphon into clean plastic screwtop bottles.
- Store in a cool place for 4/5 days after which the ginger beer will be ready to drink.

SAFETY!
Use plastic bottles as sometimes the build-up of gas can cause glass bottles to explode.

Sterilised plastic bucket and lid.

- Try making your own ginger beer from your own recipe: ground ginger, yeast, sugar, lemon juice, water.

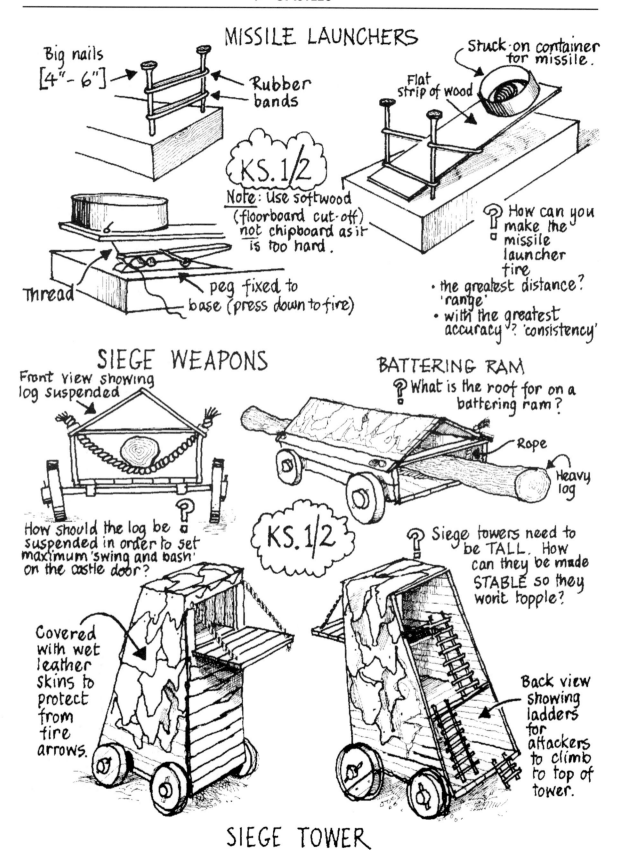

MISSILE LAUNCHERS

Big nails [4"– 6"] → Rubber bands

Stuck on container for missile.

Flat strip of wood

KS.1/2

Note: Use softwood (floorboard cut-off) not chipboard as it is too hard.

Thread

peg fixed to base (press down to fire)

? How can you make the missile launcher fire
• the greatest distance? 'range'
• with the greatest accuracy? 'consistency'

SIEGE WEAPONS

Front view showing log suspended

How should the log be suspended in order to set maximum 'swing and bash' on the castle door?

BATTERING RAM

? What is the roof for on a battering ram?

Rope

Heavy log

KS.1/2

? Siege towers need to be TALL. How can they be made STABLE so they won't topple?

Covered with wet leather skins to protect from fire arrows.

Back view showing ladders for attackers to climb to top of tower.

SIEGE TOWER

28

WATER ROCKET

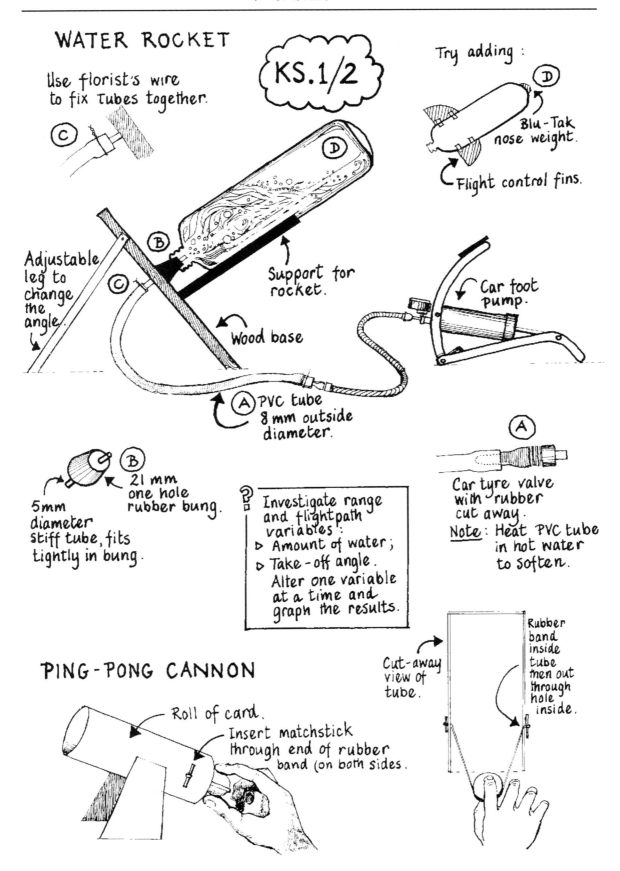

Use florist's wire to fix tubes together.
Ⓒ

KS.1/2

Try adding:
Ⓓ
Blu-Tak nose weight.
Flight control fins.

Ⓓ

Ⓑ

Support for rocket.

Adjustable leg to change the angle.

Ⓒ

Wood base

Car foot pump.

Ⓐ PVC tube 8 mm outside diameter.

Ⓐ

5mm diameter stiff tube, fits tightly in bung.

Ⓑ 21 mm one hole rubber bung.

Car tyre valve with rubber cut away.
Note: Heat PVC tube in hot water to soften.

Investigate range and flightpath variables:
▷ Amount of water;
▷ Take-off angle.
   Alter one variable at a time and graph the results.

PING-PONG CANNON

Roll of card.
Insert matchstick through end of rubber band (on both sides.

Cut-away view of tube.

Rubber band inside tube then out through hole inside.

29

PUNCH AND JUDY

Winder

'Change of Scene' back drop.

Different scenes on a long roll of fabric or paper.

KS.1/2

KS.1

ROD PUPPET

Paper fasteners for pivots

Card

Stiff wire

Stiff wire To operate

Papier Mâché

Glue

Plasticine model of head.

Papier Mâché Head

Glue head on

GLOVE PUPPET

Two layers of fabric stitched together with running stitch.

When hard, cut in half (teachers job) and remove plasticine Seal back together with papier mâché.

PICNIC FOOD

Squeezer

Blender

FRUIT JUICE:
- Choose a piece of citrus fruit (orange, lemon;
- Squeeze out juice or cut into pieces and put in a blender;
- Add honey or sugar to taste;
- Shake;
- Strain and serve.

KS. 1/2

DRINKS CAN 'COOLBOX'

Carrying loop

CHARLIE

Card carpetroll

Surface decoration

End closed off

SANDWICHES

- Choose healthy sandwich fillings:
  spreads;
  fruits;
  salads;
  eggs;
  cheese.

Vacuum flask. Keeps drinks hot or cold.

PICNIC HAMPER
KS.2

Cardboard box

Insulate floor, walls, and lid. (Use foil, foam, or bubble pack.)

BEACH BAG
KS.2

Stitch hems for drawstrings.

Hand grip.

Shoulder strap.

Plastic sheets (or fabric lined with plastic).

Note: plastic on the outside because it's turned inside out after stitching.

31

BOATS

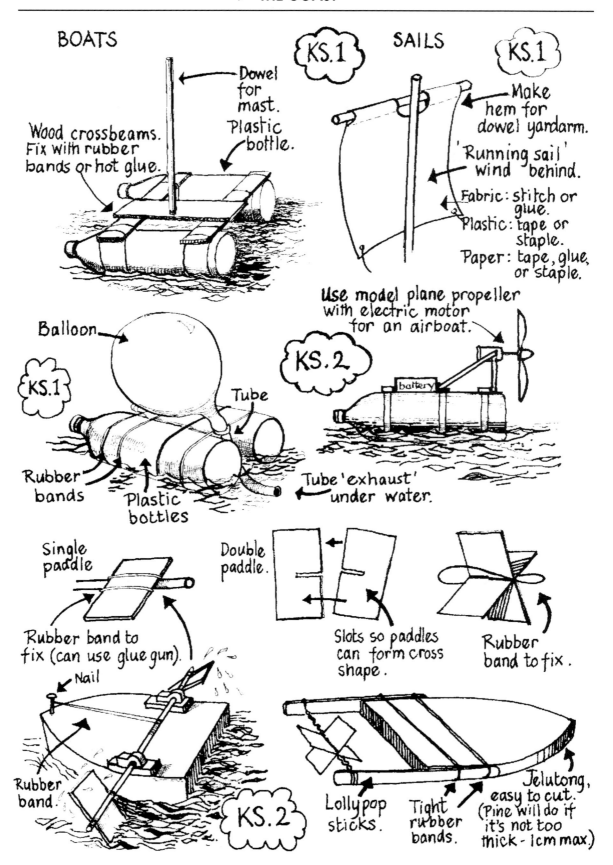

SAILS

KS.1

KS.1

Dowel for mast. Plastic bottle.

Wood crossbeams. Fix with rubber bands or hot glue.

Make hem for dowel yardarm.

'Running sail' wind behind.

Fabric: stitch or glue.
Plastic: tape or staple.
Paper: tape, glue, or staple.

Balloon

KS.1

Use model plane propeller with electric motor for an airboat.

KS.2

battery

Tube

Rubber bands

Plastic bottles

Tube 'exhaust' under water.

Single paddle

Double paddle.

Rubber band to fix (can use glue gun).

Slots so paddles can form cross shape.

Rubber band to fix.

Nail

Rubber band.

KS.2

Lollypop sticks.

Tight rubber bands.

Jelutong, easy to cut. (Pine will do if it's not too thick - 1cm max)

32

ROUNDABOUT

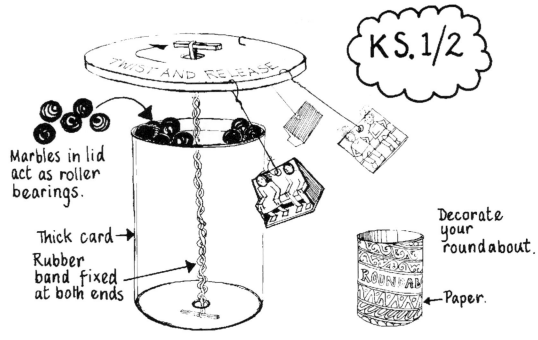

KS.1/2

Marbles in lid act as roller bearings.

Thick card →

Rubber band fixed at both ends

Decorate your roundabout.

←Paper.

HELTER SKELTER

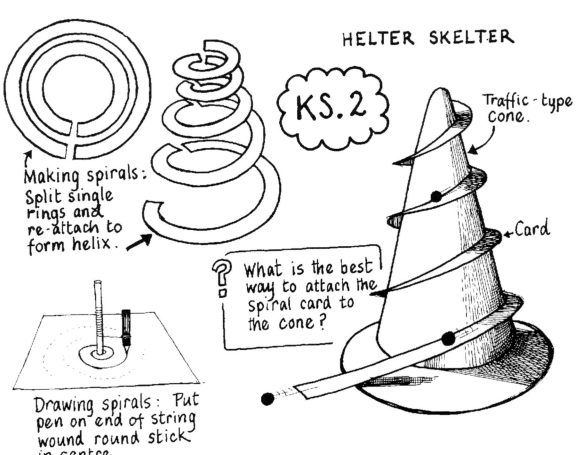

KS.2

Making spirals: Split single rings and re-attach to form helix.

? What is the best way to attach the spiral card to the cone?

Traffic-type cone.

←Card

Drawing spirals: Put pen on end of string wound round stick in centre.

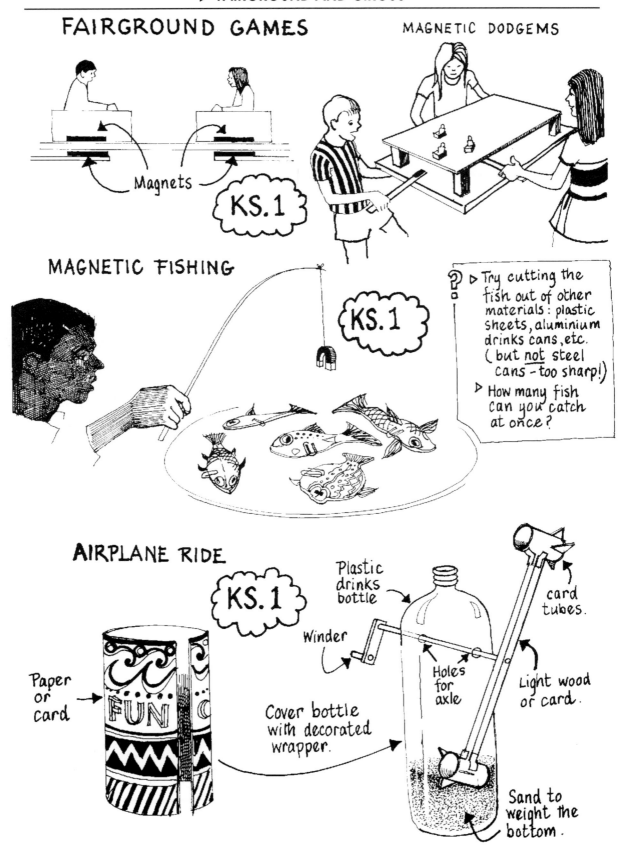

FAIRGROUND GAMES

MAGNETIC DODGEMS

Magnets

KS.1

MAGNETIC FISHING

KS.1

? ▷ Try cutting the fish out of other materials: plastic sheets, aluminium drinks cans, etc. (but not steel cans – too sharp!)

▷ How many fish can you catch at once?

AIRPLANE RIDE

KS.1

Paper or card

Plastic drinks bottle

card tubes.

Winder

Holes for axle

Light wood or card.

Cover bottle with decorated wrapper.

Sand to weight the bottom.

FAIRGROUND FOOD

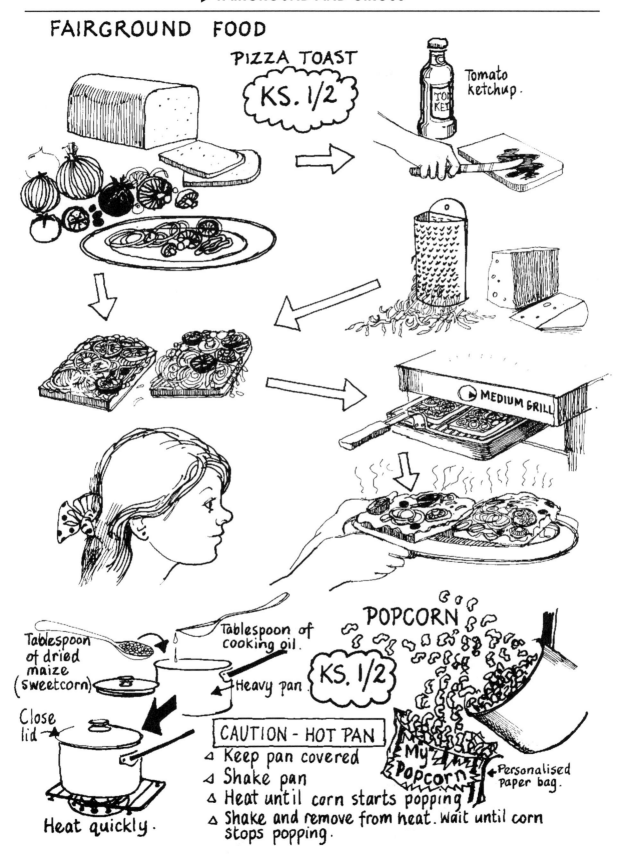

PIZZA TOAST

KS. 1/2

Tomato ketchup.

MEDIUM GRILL

Tablespoon of dried maize (sweetcorn)

Tablespoon of cooking oil.

Heavy pan.

Close lid

Heat quickly.

POPCORN

KS. 1/2

My Popcorn

Personalised paper bag.

CAUTION - HOT PAN
△ Keep pan covered
△ Shake pan
△ Heat until corn starts popping
△ Shake and remove from heat. Wait until corn stops popping.

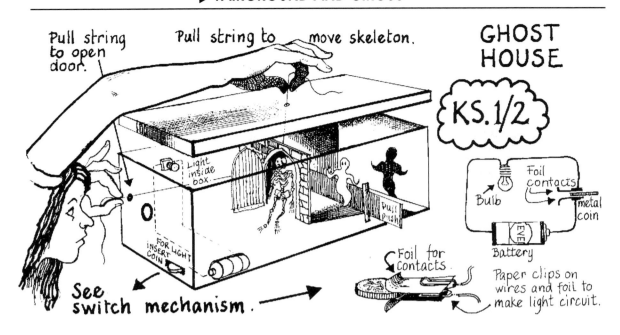

Pull string to open door.

Pull string to move skeleton.

GHOST HOUSE

KS.1/2

Light inside box.

FOR LIGHT INSERT COIN

See switch mechanism.

Pull Push

Bulb

Foil contacts

metal coin

Battery

Foil for contacts.

Paper clips on wires and foil to make light circuit.

COLOUR WHEEL SPINNERS

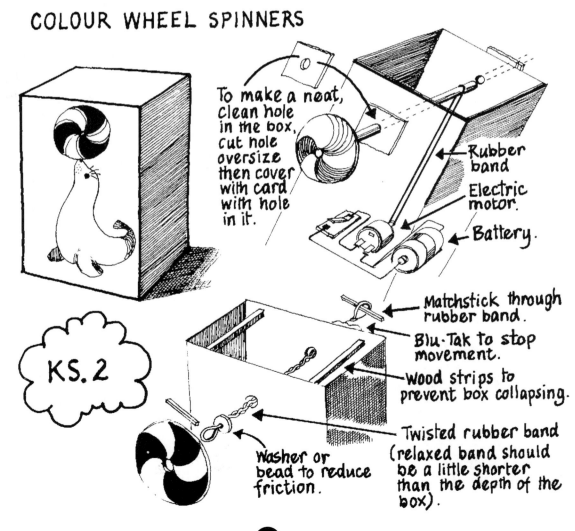

To make a neat, clean hole in the box, cut hole oversize then cover with card with hole in it.

Rubber band

Electric motor.

Battery.

Matchstick through rubber band.

Blu-Tak to stop movement.

Wood strips to prevent box collapsing.

KS.2

Washer or bead to reduce friction.

Twisted rubber band (relaxed band should be a little shorter than the depth of the box).

MAKE YOUR OWN CLOWN OUTFIT

KS.2

Face paints

Velcro for 'opening'

MAKING POM-POMS

Wind wool around two card rings.

Cut wool round outside of 'doughnut'

Separate rings and tie wool tightly between them.

Pom-pom button.

MAKE A PATTERN
▷ Lie on the floor.
▷ Ask someone to draw round you (leave room for seams).
▷ Stitch the two layers together.

ANIMATED CLOWN FACE

card

Rear view

Guides

KS.1/2

Tab

Push/pull tab to move eyes and ears.

Eyes and ears on moving strip (tab)

THE JUGGLER

Disguise paper fastener as part of the design. (nose)

KS.1/2

Paper fastener

Rear view

card disc

WIND SPINNERS

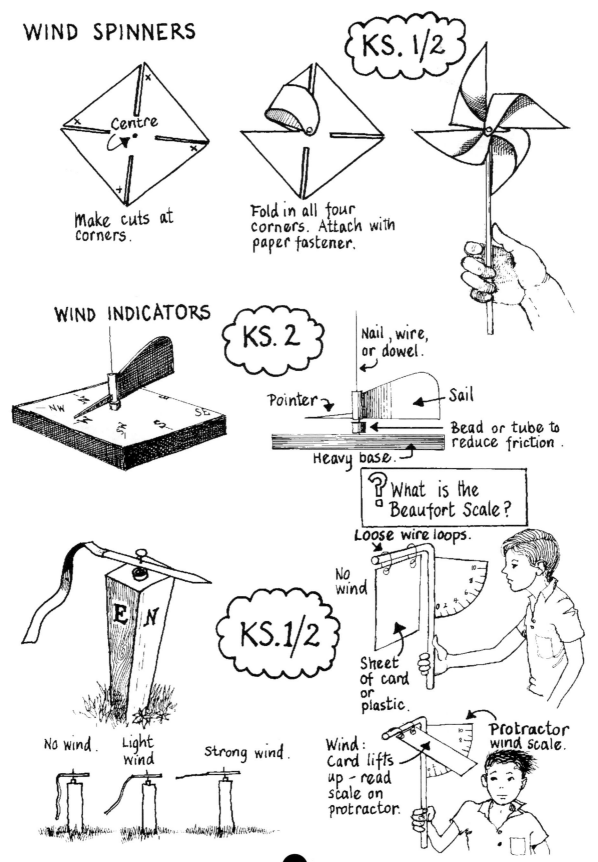

KS. 1/2

Centre

Make cuts at corners.

Fold in all four corners. Attach with paper fastener.

WIND INDICATORS

KS. 2

Nail, wire, or dowel.

Pointer

Sail

Bead or tube to reduce friction.

Heavy base.

? What is the Beaufort Scale?

Loose wire loops.

No wind

Sheet of card or plastic.

KS. 1/2

No wind.   Light Wind   Strong wind.

Wind: Card lifts up - read scale on protractor.

Protractor wind scale.

WINDMILLS

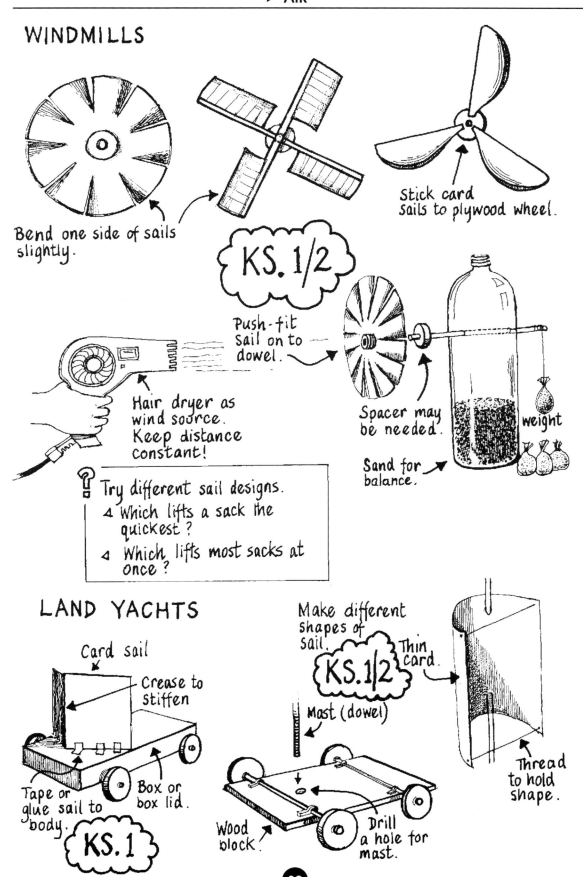

Bend one side of sails slightly.

Stick card sails to plywood wheel.

KS. 1/2

Push-fit sail on to dowel.

Hair dryer as wind source. Keep distance constant!

Spacer may be needed.

weight

Sand for balance.

? Try different sail designs.
◁ Which lifts a sack the quickest?
◁ Which lifts most sacks at once?

LAND YACHTS

Card sail

Crease to stiffen

Tape or glue sail to body.

Box or box lid.

KS.1

Make different shapes of sail.

KS.1/2

Thin card.

Mast (dowel)

Wood block.

Drill a hole for mast.

Thread to hold shape.

MAKING KITES

A4 Paper

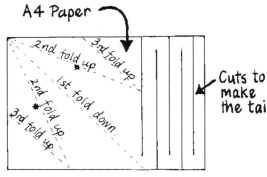

2nd fold up
3rd fold up
2nd fold up
1st fold down
2nd fold up
3rd fold up

Cuts to make the tail.

* Bridle fixing points: use a small piece of tape to attach cotton bridle.

INVESTIGATIONS

▷ How small a piece of paper can you use to make an Alanya kite?

▷ Try different patterns of tail cuts: thinner, thicker, curved, or spiral.

ALANYA INDOOR KITE

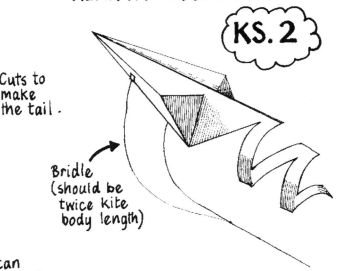

KS.2

Bridle (should be twice kite body length)

SKY 1

Decorate your kite.

Ratio of sizes

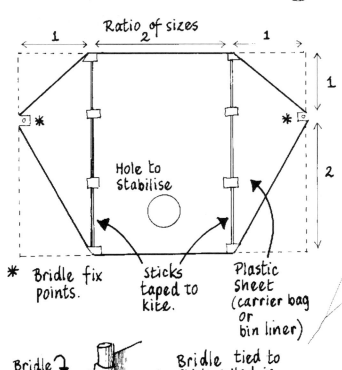

1   2   1

1

2

Hole to stabilise

* Bridle fix points.

Sticks taped to kite.

Plastic Sheet (carrier bag or bin liner)

Bridle

Thin stick.

Bridle tied to stick rolled in corner of kite.

SLED KITE

Bridle (should be twice kite body length)

KS.2

BLINDS AND CURTAINS

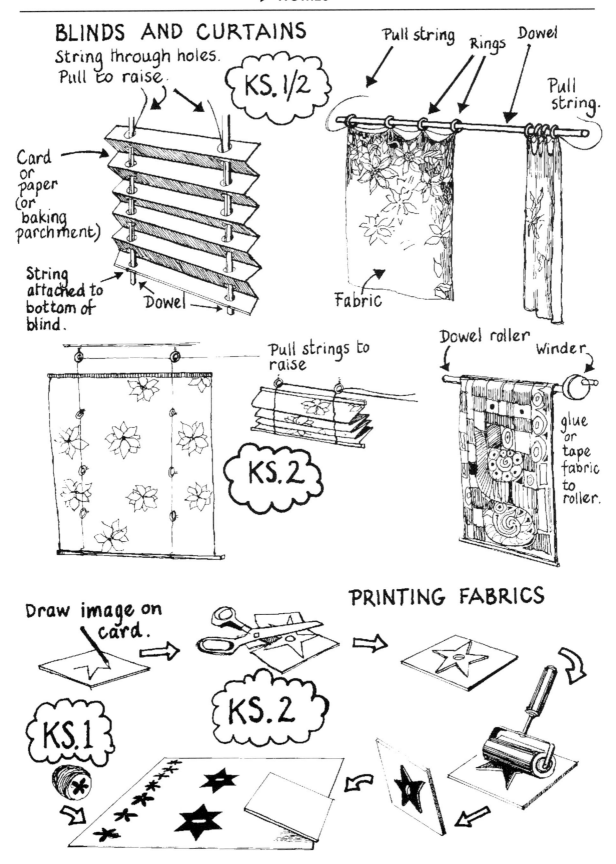

String through holes.
Pull to raise.

KS. 1/2

Card
or
paper
(or
baking
parchment)

String
attached to
bottom of
blind.

Dowel

Pull string

Rings

Dowel

Pull
string.

Fabric

Pull strings to
raise

KS. 2

Dowel roller

Winder

glue
or
tape
fabric
to
roller.

PRINTING FABRICS

Draw image on
card.

KS.1

KS.2

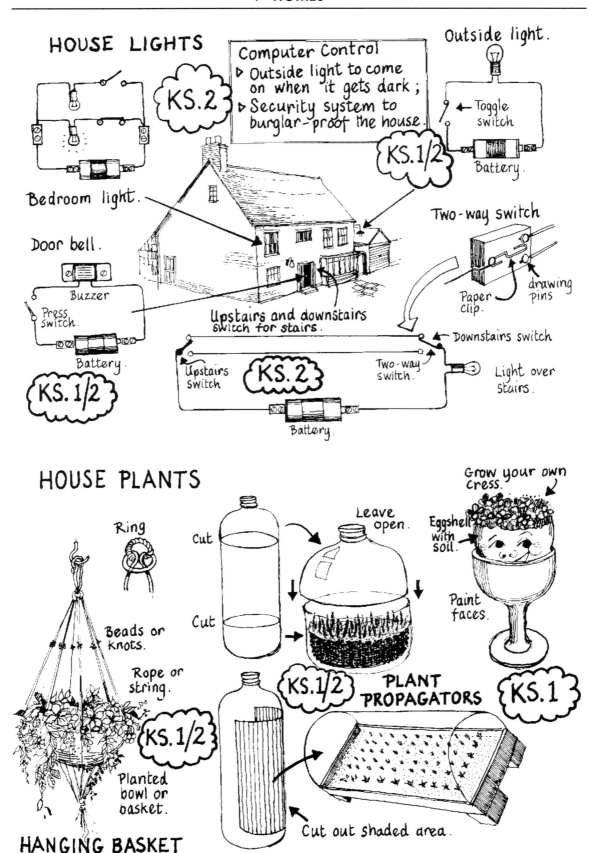

HOUSE LIGHTS

KS.2

Computer Control
▷ Outside light to come on when it gets dark;
▷ Security system to burglar-proof the house.

KS.1/2

Outside light.

Toggle switch

Battery.

Bedroom light.

Door bell.

Buzzer

Press switch.

Battery.

KS.1/2

Two-way switch

Paper clip.

drawing pins

Upstairs and downstairs switch for stairs.

Upstairs Switch

KS.2

Two-way switch.

Downstairs switch

Light over stairs.

Battery.

HOUSE PLANTS

Ring

Cut

Cut

Leave open.

Grow your own cress.

Eggshell with soil.

Paint faces.

KS.1

Beads or knots.

Rope or string.

KS.1/2

KS.1/2

PLANT PROPAGATORS

Planted bowl or basket.

Cut out shaded area.

HANGING BASKET

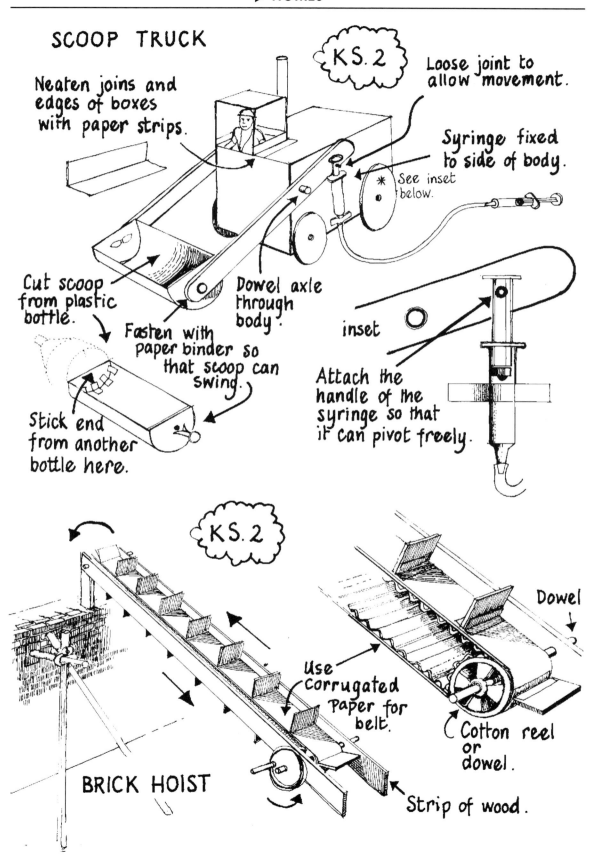

SCOOP TRUCK

KS.2

Neaten joins and edges of boxes with paper strips.

Loose joint to allow movement.

Syringe fixed to side of body.

* See inset below.

Cut scoop from plastic bottle.

Dowel axle through body.

Fasten with paper binder so that scoop can swing.

inset

Attach the handle of the syringe so that it can pivot freely.

Stick end from another bottle here.

KS.2

BRICK HOIST

Use corrugated paper for belt.

Dowel

Cotton reel or dowel.

Strip of wood.

BUILDING SITE MACHINERY

HOOK LIFT TRUCK

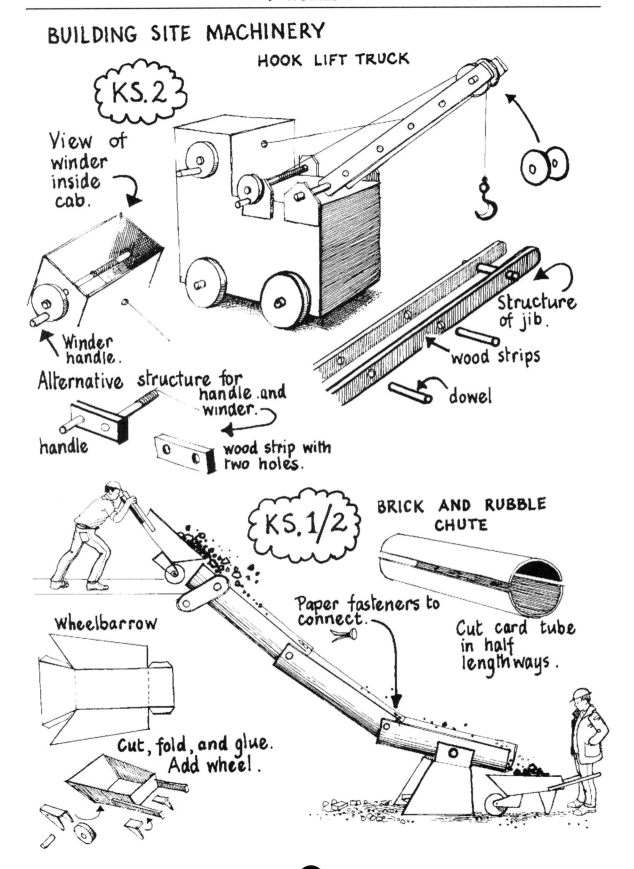

KS.2

View of winder inside cab.

Winder handle.

Structure of jib.

wood strips

dowel

Alternative structure for handle and winder.

handle

wood strip with two holes.

KS.1/2

BRICK AND RUBBLE CHUTE

Paper fasteners to connect.

Cut card tube in half lengthways.

Wheelbarrow

Cut, fold, and glue. Add wheel.

PART FOUR

TECHNOLOGY RESOURCE SHEETS

4:1 USING CONSTRUCTION MATERIALS

Building sand castles

From infancy, children respond to the materials in their environment by making things, e.g. sand castles, dens, towers of building bricks, dams in streams. Through these activities children begin to develop an understanding of materials and their properties in order that they may be used to create something. Design and technology in school builds on and extends these early experiences, refining the way in which materials are used in order that the things which are made progress from the imaginative responses of the five year old to the functional designs which are created in response to specific needs at higher levels of attainment.

The range of materials provided for the children will have an influence on the work which is produced, and so the range should be neither so narrow as to constrain ideas, nor so broad that the children are unable to develop appropriate skills in using them. Children's creative responses must not be subsumed in the struggle to manipulate the material; the craft problems must not overwhelm the design.

Some of the materials found in a primary school require sophisticated working techniques to use them to advantage, e.g. strip wood and card triangles (see below). It is important that the range of materials offered to the children progresses in line with their ability to work them.

Using recycled waste materials is a good way of starting design and technology because there is very little cost involved. In the past, 'junk modelling' has been accorded a low status in school, particularly before technology was recognised as an important part of children's experience. If we can abandon the title 'junk modelling' and refer to the activity as using 'recycled materials' we may find our expectations of what can be achieved may rise, too. In fact, recycling provides a source of good quality materials, and with some techniques for dealing with them, the resulting work can be of an excellent quality.

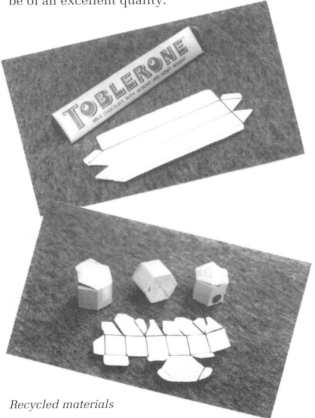

Recycled materials

To avoid storage problems, it is a good idea to make some early decisions about the potential usefulness of the materials which are saved. Not everything destined for the dustbin is going to be useful for technological work and it is important to develop a critical eye for things you know to be useful and things which you think may be useful. This is an ability that the children can develop, too.

If recycled waste materials are to provide a valuable resource, the way in which they are stored must reflect this.

On the following pages, we discuss the selection and management of materials, both bought and recycled, and describe techniques for working with them. As well as the broad categories of materials which we describe, familiar classroom materials such as leather, string, clay, balloons, marbles, paper clips and art materials also have their contributions to make to design and technology activities. (See Appendix 2 for a suggested range of other components.)

▶ Card

The wide assortment of boxes in which household commodities are packaged can provide an excellent basis for children's models and these should be readily accessible to the children, stored perhaps on a shelf or a resource table where they will not get damaged. Discard any that are torn or crushed; quality work is unlikely to result from them. Shoe boxes and the larger cereal boxes are particularly useful as they are made usually from good-quality, strong card. Detergent-powder boxes are unsuitable as usually they are waxed and are difficult to paint. In addition, powder remaining in them can cause eye irritation.

Try to provide a range of boxes with interesting shapes; for young children, making models is often a very imaginative experience, and an interestingly shaped box may provide the stimulus for a creative response.

Surplus boxes may be opened out and stored flat, to be reassembled when they are required.

Boxes and shapes for maths

This way they take up much less room and do not get crushed and damaged. A hot-glue gun is the best tool for this task and, as the glue sets almost immediately, a box can be reassembled in seconds. The adhesive PVA can also be used, but it takes much longer to dry. Hot-melt glue guns raise some health and safety issues which are discussed in Part 2, page 15.

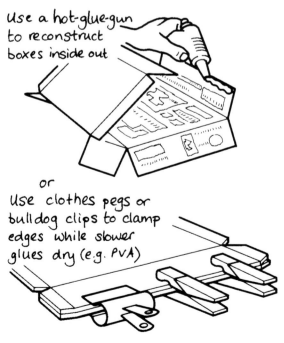

Use a hot-glue-gun to reconstruct boxes inside out

or
Use clothes pegs or bulldog clips to clamp edges while slower glues dry (e.g. PVA)

Fig.1

This process of reassembling boxes can be used to introduce the idea that 3-D forms can be developed from 2-D shapes, and encourages the use of a mathematical vocabulary for describing shapes, e.g. faces, edges, corners or vertices. Discuss the shapes of the faces that make the net of the box, and show the children how flaps are necessary to join two edges together. As the children become more familiar with the idea of developing nets they will be able to construct their own shapes if an appropriate one is not available on the resource table.

Much of the packaging of household items is brightly decorated and designed to stand out from the supermarket shelves and attract the customer's eye. Children have difficulty concealing this decoration with ordinary school paint. If, when the boxes are reassembled, they are turned inside out, thus concealing the decoration on the inside and exposing a plain surface to the outside, it is much easier to paint the model successfully.

Where the joins are made, there may be gaps which are unsightly. These may be concealed by gluing strips of very thin paper across the join. This needs to be done carefully and it is worth encouraging the children to cut strips of, say, a ruler's width. Where the join is at an edge, fold the strip in half lengthways before applying the glue. Ordinary white PVA is fine for this. When the model is painted, the paper will not be seen and the finished model will be much stiffer and neater.

This technique is especially useful when children are covering the sides of timber-framed structures with card when gaps along the edges are inevitable (see Fig. 2).

The larger faces of torn boxes may be used to provide rectangles of good quality card for a variety of purposes. Cut and square them up on a trimmer. The backs of greeting cards can be used in the same way. Local printing and packaging firms often are quite willing for schools to have their card offcuts.

When large sheets of card are used, as in, say, a mask, the card may be stiffened in much the same way as an engineer will stiffen a sheet of steel. Use a cutter to provide strips of card, and use PVA to fix the strips edge-on to the back of the sheet. This forms a kind of beam structure which provides the stiffness to prevent the card bending.

Strips of thin paper glued across joins

PVA adhesive

Cut each strip to a ruler's width and fold in half lengthways so the crease makes a neat corner

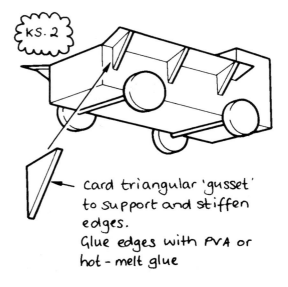

KS.2

card triangular 'gusset' to support and stiffen edges.
Glue edges with PVA or hot-melt glue

Fig.2

Fig.3

If card is to be folded, as in the construction of nets, children should be taught how to score the card so that they can achieve a clean fold. A safety ruler and the point of a pair of scissors do this perfectly; craft knives cut too deeply into the card.

If card is being folded to create a hinge, it may be more useful to use the hinge created by the lid of a box or the fold of a greeting card. Here the fold has been punched by a machine rather than scored by hand and the material has not been weakened by a cutting action.

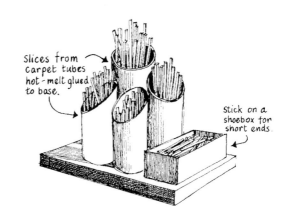

Slices from carpet tubes hot-melt glued to base.

Stick on a shoebox for short ends.

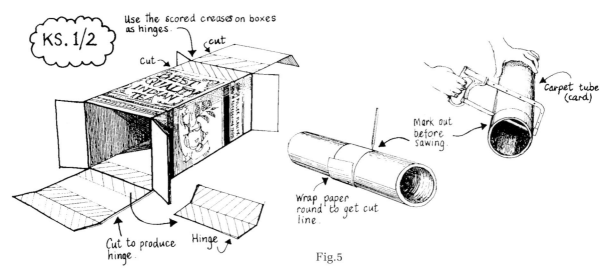

KS. 1/2

Use the scored creases on boxes as hinges.

cut

Cut

Cut to produce hinge.

Hinge

Carpet tube (card)

Mark out before sawing.

Wrap paper round to get cut line.

Fig.5

or use the fold of a greetings card for a hinge.

Cut

MERRY CHRISTMAS

Fig.4

The cardboard tubes on which carpet or cushion floor is rolled are useful if you can saw them up into short lengths. Put some in the resources stock and use others to create storage systems for wood, dowel and metal rods.

▶ *WOOD*

Balsa

The main value of balsa wood is its extreme lightness which makes it a most suitable material for gliders and other flying objects.

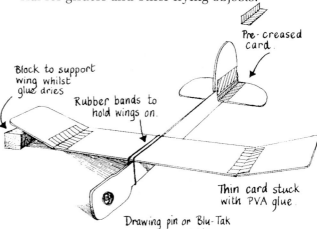

Pre-creased card.

Block to support wing whilst glue dries

Rubber bands to hold wings on.

Thin card stuck with PVA glue.

Drawing pin or Blu-Tak as a nose weight.

Fig.6

Traditionally, balsa cement is used for joining pieces of balsa together. It is a quick setting glue but its solvent base makes it unsuitable for children's use. If the surfaces to be joined are flat, PVA makes an excellent bond. Strips of thin card or paper glued over a join will dry almost as quickly as balsa cement and be as strong.

For general construction purposes, there are better materials than balsa and because of its cost, its use is best restricted to those occasions when weight is a significant factor in the design. The boxes of mixed sizes of balsa pieces tend to be a poor economy since the thicker sections usually remain unused. If your main use for balsa is for flight projects, then a box of sheet balsa may be a better buy.

Square Section Timber and Card Triangles

8 mm and 10 mm square sections of timber can be used to construct frames for models. The extra rigidity that this type of construction provides is ideal if the model is to incorporate moving parts and has to withstand greater stress.

In this technique, the strips of wood are joined together using card triangles and PVA. The glue is applied to the card and positioned over the join between two pieces of wood. A triangle should be glued to each side of the join.

If the framework is to be rectangular, right angled triangles should be used and a guide of centimetre squared paper laid beneath the construction will help.

Extra reinforcement may be provided by gluing thin strips of card to the inside corner made by two pieces of wood.

3-D structures can also be made using this method. To join a vertical strip of wood to a frame, larger triangles may be folded in half and glued to the base to provide a perpendicular support to the vertical strip which may then be reinforced by the addition of strips of card.

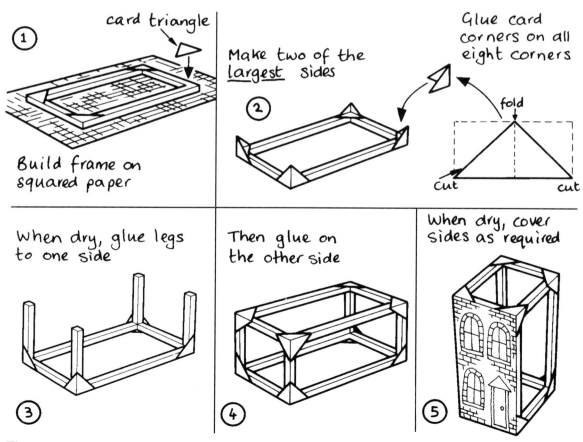

Fig.7

When large structures are made, there will be a problem of rigidity and some form of bracing will be necessary. Working with geo-strips will lead children towards an understanding of the need for triangulation of structures which will help them in their constructions.

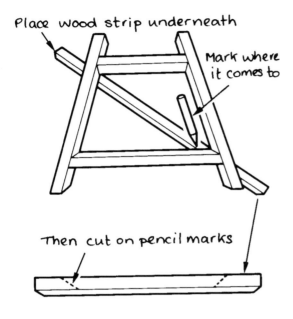

Place wood strip underneath

Mark where it comes to

Then cut on pencil marks

Fig.8

To fit a diagonal brace in the rectangular face of a wood frame structure, the best way is to hold a length of wood behind the structure and to mark the position where the pieces of wood overlap. This is more accurate than measuring in standard units and provides the correct angle at which to make the cut.

The timber called jelutong is widely available from educational suppliers. This is a soft wood with a fine grain which does not splinter. But it is quite expensive and like balsa is a tropical wood, the use of which we should reconsider for ecological reasons. The fast-growing northern timbers, such as pine and fir, are quite adequate and cheaper.

DIY stores often stock the small sections of wood though it is sometimes a much harder wood than either pine or jelutong and small children may experience difficulty in cutting it.

Other Methods of Joining Wood

Nailing or screwing wood together is not really appropriate for the small sections of wood commonly found in the primary classroom. The wood will usually split if attempts are made to drive even small pins or screws in, unless great skill is exercised, particularly when the join is made at the end of a piece of wood.

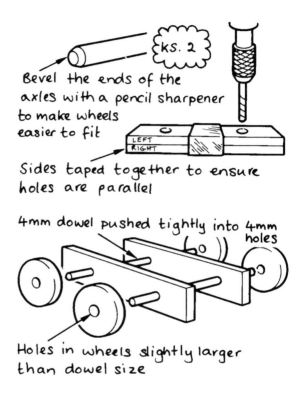

ks. 2

Bevel the ends of the axles with a pencil sharpener to make wheels easier to fit

LEFT
RIGHT

Sides taped together to ensure holes are parallel

4mm dowel pushed tightly into 4mm holes

Holes in wheels slightly larger than dowel size

Fig.9

Dowelling joints are very effective when used with larger sections of wood (at least 1 cm wide). To make a ladder-like construction, two suitable pieces of wood may be taped together, and holes (of a size to make a tight fit with a piece of dowel) drilled through both pieces together. Lengths of dowel then may be cut to join the two pieces of wood to make a very rigid frame which can be dismantled if required. If there is any difficulty pushing the dowel into the holes, turn the end of the dowel *once* in a pencil sharpener to give it a slightly bevelled shape, and it will push more easily into the hold. This will provide a very rigid structure. Dowel pegs can be used to make a concealed join between two pieces of wood.

Making models from wood can work out rather costly. If you have a group of children making a vehicle, for example, it is sensible to select appropriate boxes for the body and to build a frame as a chassis to fit the boxes instead of constructing the whole thing from wood; a much more time consuming and costly approach. There will be occasions when boxes are not rigid enough to support moving parts and a frame will need to be constructed to accommodate, for example, gears or pulleys.

When using wood there are some skills which the children will need to be taught. For example, the wood to be cut must always be held securely using any of the items listed below:

A junior hacksaw is an appropriate tool to use for sawing small sections of wood. Make sure the blade is in the correct position with the teeth pointing away from the handle so that the cutting action is on the push stroke, otherwise you will find that the wood is pulled away from the stop on the bench hook with each sawing action. If the children experience any difficulty sawing, it may be as a result of applying too much force, in which case the blades may become bent.

If the children are cutting pieces of wood which are too large to fit on the bench hook or in a jig, then a small G-clamp may be used to anchor the work securely to the table.

Fig.10 *Using a junior hacksaw*   Fig.11 *Using a gents saw*

- a **cutting board** is designed to hook over the table edge and the wood to be cut is held firmly with one hand whilst the other is used for sawing;
- small **cutting jigs** are also available which are designed to hold specific sizes of wood. The jig must be held in a small vice;
- **vices** are available quite cheaply and may be used effectively to hold pieces of wood without a cutting jig;
- **G-clamps** are cheap and invaluable for steadying work whilst it is being cut.

A junior hacksaw is not always suitable for larger sections of wood as the space between the blade and the back of the saw is small. A gent's saw should be used to cut larger sheets of wood, which should be firmly clamped to, and overhanging, the edge of the table. Small children will have difficulty cutting large sheets of material easily and accurately, and sometimes it may be appropriate for the teacher to help. A tenon saw may be used for this job, but it is larger and less well suited to the size of primary school children.

Fix work on table.

Use saw gently up and down; use full length of blade.

Often easier to kneel down.

Fig. 12 *Using a coping saw*

If a curved cut is required then a coping saw should be used. The coping saw blade can be turned as it moves around the curve. A shaper saw is a mains-operated tool which is safe for primary children to use and will do the same job with rather less effort. (See Appendix 1 for more information on choosing and using tools.)

A collection of wood offcuts is always useful, but take care not to provide a selection of offcuts whose dimensions are so great as to make them unworkable for young children. Be selective about the contents; short lengths of board (e.g. ply, pine, chipboard, blockboard and hardboard) make useful bases.

▶ *Metal*

There are few metals which can be used safely with young children. Metals are often difficult to manipulate because of their qualities of toughness, stiffness and hardness which make them so useful in the adult world. Joining metal to metal requires the use of tools and techniques few of which are suitable for primary children. Tinplate (of which food cans are made) can have knife-like edges which can inflict a nasty wound, although metals formed into the thin sheets we know as foil are useful.

Some drinks cans are made of thin aluminium (others are tinplate and can be identified with a magnet) which can easily be cut with utility snips (this is a job for the teacher). This provides a supply of flat metal strips which can be particularly useful for their property as good electrical conductors in switches, for example. Aluminium cooking foil, and the more robust foil food containers are useful for their conductive and reflective properties.

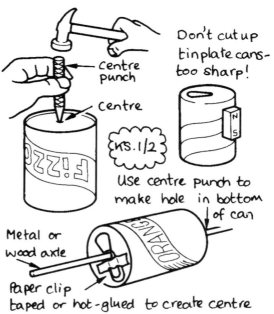

Centre punch

centre

Don't cut up tinplate cans - too sharp!

KS.1/2

Use centre punch to make hole in bottom of can

Metal or wood axle

Paper clip taped or hot-glued to create centre

Fig.13

Drinks cans are a good source of rollers for vehicles. Using a centre punch (or if this is not available, a nail) a hole can be made in the base of the can. The further you drive in the centre punch the larger the hole will be, so it is important to decide first of all what is to be used as an axle. The hole must be located centrally if the roller is to roll smoothly and this provides the children with an interesting mathematical problem; just how do you find the centre of a circle? The top of the can will already have a hole made by the ring pull, and this needs reducing to a size appropriate to the size of the axle which is to be used. There are several ways of doing this, some of which are described here. Before the roller is fixed onto a model, spin it on an axle to make sure that it rotates evenly and adjust the centre accordingly.

Wire coat-hangers are a useful source of axles, particularly when used with drinks can rollers where the metal-to-metal contact has a low frictional resistance and runs smoothly. Use a junior hacksaw to cut off the straight lengths of the coat-hanger and store the pieces in a length of cardboard tube or plastic drainpipe. Coat-hangers can also be used as frames for weaving.

▶ Plastics

A wide range of plastic materials can be salvaged and put to good use. This material is likely to be used in the form in which you find it because plastics are shaped by industrial processes most of which are inaccessible and too dangerous for young children. Plastics come in two kinds:

- **thermoplastics**, which go soft when heated, can be shaped in various ways and retain this shape when cooled. Perspex is one of these plastics. Many plastic containers and items like washing-up bowls are made this way, which is why they collapse so spectacularly when overheated. The softening temperature varies between different plastics but can be as low as 100 °C, or even lower in the case of some plastic teaspoons;

- **thermoset plastics** which are moulded into a form when first made and cannot be softened and reshaped. Bakelite was the first of these, invented a surprisingly long time ago. The gear-lever knob on the 1916 Rolls Royce is alleged to be the first commercial use. These plastics, widely used in electrical fittings and saucepan handles, burn rather than soften when heated and give off that characteristic smell.

Plastic lids make excellent wheels if a piece of wood is glued across the diameter of the lid, and drilled to fit tightly onto a piece of dowel. Hot glue will have to be used for this job; PVA does not stick onto plastics because they are non-absorbent. Contact adhesives (e.g. Evo-stick) stick well but are usually solvent-based and so are potentially dangerous. Metal lids can be turned into wheels in the same way.

Cotton reels make useful wheels, particularly when fitted with tyres made from pipe insulation.

Buy foam from DIY stores in 1.5 metre lengths and cut with a bread knife

Buggy wheels: foam pipe-insulation on a cotton reel

Wood to hold axle on coffee jar lid

Fig.14

Washing-up-liquid bottles are useful as an air source for inflating balloons which are providing the lift in a model. The nozzles should be collected as they can substitute for beads to reduce friction between rotating surfaces.

Margarine and ice-cream tubs, and some of the flat-sided liquid containers are made of a plastic which feels slippery to the touch. This material can easily be cut with utility snips and it is worth saving the larger flat areas as they have many uses. A small sheet of this material with a hole punched in it, placed between two moving surfaces in a box model, for example, will provide a low friction surface on which the movement can take place. Its properties as an electrical insulator, and its natural springiness are also potentially useful.

Corriflute is a plastic version of corrugated card. It is brightly coloured, very light and strong. It is quite an expensive material to use and it is sensible to encourage the children to make patterns from card or paper before using the plastic to avoid waste. When used as a vehicle chassis the corrugations in the plastic may be used as axle bearings. A metal rod makes a very free-running axle in this situation.

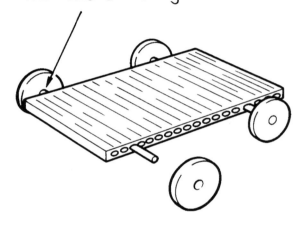

Coloured corrugated plastic sheet (Corriflute) can be used for vehicle bodies.
The holes can carry the axles

Fig.15

The most suitable method for cutting corriflute is to use a craft knife with a safety rule, although utility snips will probably be a safer alternative for young children. Hot-melt glue will stick pieces of corroflute together; self adhesive foam pads are a less successful alternative. Rivets designed to be used with this material may be used to create box-like structures. The problems of cutting and joining this material may exclude it from many primary classrooms.

Perspex is a material widely used in secondary schools, but not so useful at primary level where the processes involved in shaping the material require specialist equipment and a heat source. Most commonly, perspex is formed into interesting shapes by heating and bending. Once the perspex cools it retains its new shape.

Perspex can be cut with a junior hacksaw and drilled quite easily provided the surface is masked with tape to prevent slipping of the drill. Small chips of perspex can fly out from the drill tip so safety spectacles should be worn and other children kept clear. There are special adhesives available which allow perspex to be joined, although some of these are not suitable for children's use. Perspex and similar hard plastics should not be rubbed with abrasive paper because hazardous dust is created.

As part of the development of children's understanding of materials allow them to investigate properties such as flexibility, strength, scratch resistance or buoyancy. Do not try burning plastics; most burn at high temperatures and give off vast amounts of foul and toxic smoke.

▶ *Rubber*

Bicycle inner tubes are a useful source of rubber bands which can be cut to any width; a useful source of 'tyres' to improve the grip of wheels.

▶ *Environmental Issues*

While developing awareness of materials and their properties, and learning to use them, children should be developing awareness of the social issues relating to these materials. The rapid depletion of the world's resources and the pressing problems of disposal are inseparable from consideration of the materials themselves. The very qualities that make materials so useful (such as the resistance to biodegradation of plastics) often create the most intractable difficulties (the permanence of plastics litter). The recycling of materials is a good example of changing public awareness and one which young children can understand and practice.

4:2 WORKING WITH TEXTILES

Young children usually begin to develop their skills with textiles through activities which focus on the development of aesthetic items, e.g. collage, samplers. Soon, they can progress to considering the more functional aspects of different textiles such as, how warm, waterproof or hard-wearing they are.The aesthetic qualities of textiles, their colours and textures, are important considerations whether they are being used within artwork or more functionally, such as in a garment. In reality, there is no clear division between the aesthetic and functional aspects, as a glance at fashion designs shows.

▶ Creating Yarns from Fibres

Children can create their own yarns from fleece by using simple spinning techniques. These may be used to create interesting textures for use in weaving and collage, though you might find they are not strong enough to use for knitting. It is useful and interesting for children to be involved in the process of creating a familiar material. This can also provide an opportunity to investigate the dyeing process and to make dyes from plants.

Yarns can be made very easily by using a ball of fleece or cotton wool and teasing out strands by hand, twisting at the same time to make a thread.

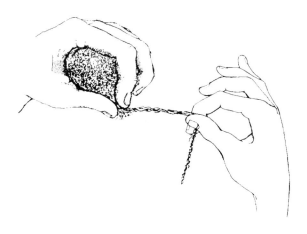

Fig.1

Brushing fleece with special wire brushes called carders helps to organise the fibres so that they lie in the same direction and so makes it easier to pull out the thread. This can be done by hand if you haven't any carders. A bundle of fleece that has been carded is called a rollag.

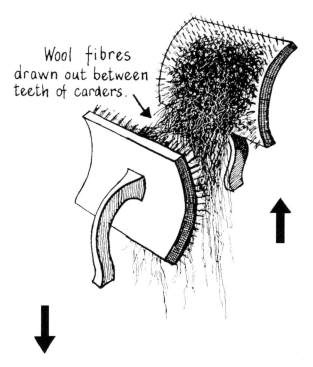

Wool fibres drawn out between teeth of carders.

Fig.2

Once you have about 50 cm yarn this can be tied around a spindle which is allowed to hang down freely. The spindle should be twisted so that it spins in an anti-clockwise direction, twisting the spun yarn to bind the fibres together; a loosely twisted yarn will pull apart easily. As it spins, more fibres should be drawn out of the rollag and allowed to twist into the yarn. From time to time the newly spun yarn can be wound around the spindle to keep the spindle from touching the floor and to keep the yarn taut (see Fig. 3).

Spinning needs plenty of practice in order to co-ordinate all these actions. If children work in pairs, one child can keep the spindle turning whilst the other pulls out the fibres. The spindle must always spin in the same direction. The yarn will almost certainly be knobbly and this interesting texture can be effective.

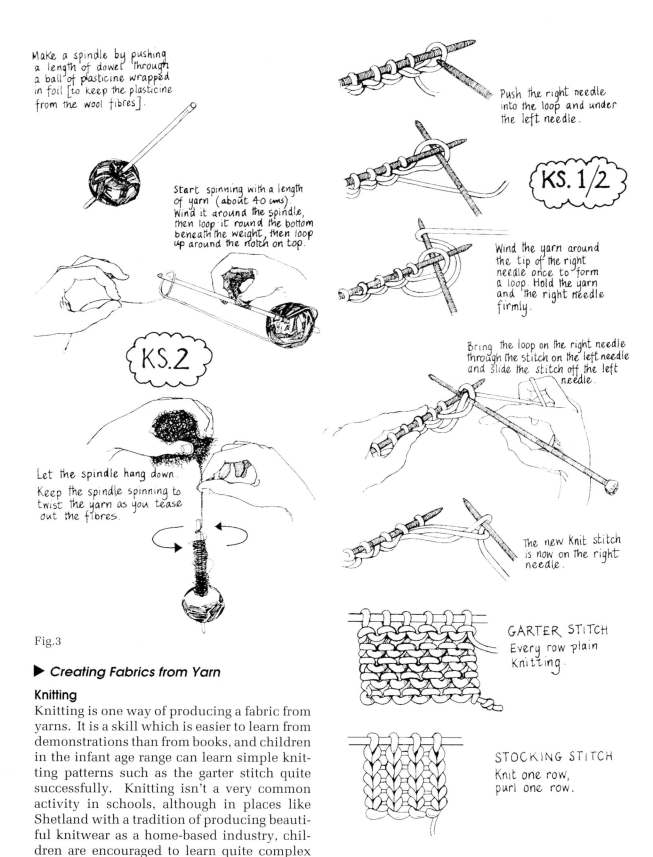

Make a spindle by pushing a length of dowel through a ball of plasticine wrapped in foil [to keep the plasticine from the wool fibres].

Start spinning with a length of yarn (about 40 cms). Wind it around the spindle, then loop it round the bottom beneath the weight, then loop up around the notch on top.

KS.2

Let the spindle hang down. Keep the spindle spinning to twist the yarn as you tease out the fibres.

Fig.3

Push the right needle into the loop and under the left needle.

KS.1/2

Wind the yarn around the tip of the right needle once to form a loop. Hold the yarn and the right needle firmly.

Bring the loop on the right needle through the stitch on the left needle and slide the stitch off the left needle.

The new knit stitch is now on the right needle.

GARTER STITCH
Every row plain knitting.

STOCKING STITCH
Knit one row, purl one row.

Fig.4

▶ Creating Fabrics from Yarn

Knitting

Knitting is one way of producing a fabric from yarns. It is a skill which is easier to learn from demonstrations than from books, and children in the infant age range can learn simple knitting patterns such as the garter stitch quite successfully. Knitting isn't a very common activity in schools, although in places like Shetland with a tradition of producing beautiful knitwear as a home-based industry, children are encouraged to learn quite complex patterns such as Fair Isle.

The younger children can begin by knitting simple strips, e.g. Teddy's scarf or squares to make a blanket for the home corner.

They can progress to using shapes such as squares and rectangles to make a variety of simple garments and other items before being introduced to the codes of knitting patterns.

Fig.5

As part of their science activities children can examine different yarns with a magnifying glass (x10 magnification is suitable) to see how the fibres intertwine.

Not all knitted fabrics use natural fibres; many are synthetic, made from chemicals derived from oil. A synthetic material which can be used for knitting is a plastic bag. Cut in a spiral fashion around the bag and the length of plastic can be knitted to create an interesting fabric. Raffia can be knitted, too.

Fig.6

Weaving

Weaving yarns is the most common way of creating fabrics. This can be introduced at a very simple level, using paper strips or weaving cards and progress to weaving on a simple home-made frame or loom.

Making a loom

Children might use these methods to produce mats, belts or small items which do not need large amounts of fabric.

Sewing

The techniques of sewing can be introduced quite early on by allowing children to make large stitches randomly on a piece of cloth so that gradually they learn control of the needle. Starting and finishing off will probably need to be done by the teacher at first. Sewn pictures or collages can be made using the tacking stitch. This is applique and can be developed by using fabrics with different textures, and incorporating new stitches as they are learned. Buttons, sequins and beads can be added too.

It is best to start by using fabrics which do not fray such as felts, net or vivelle (a paper-backed fabric). Eventually, the children can extend the range of materials by learning how to turn a hem on those materials which fray, or using a close zig-zag stitch on a sewing-machine to hold the edges.

Binca, a loosely woven canvas with large evenly spaced holes may be used to help the children make more even length stitches, and simple mats or samplers can be produced. These straight stitches can be decorated by weaving threads of different colour through each stitch.

A running stitch can be used for joining two pieces of material together allowing children to make a wider range of items.

Embroidery is one of the ways in which plain fabrics can be decorated. There are a number of simple embroidery stitches which children can learn to enhance their work. An embroidery hoop will help keep the fabric taut whilst it is being worked.

Stiffen with pipe cleaners.

Stitch, appliqué, or use felt pen.

Fabric shapes stitched into tube.

Fig.7

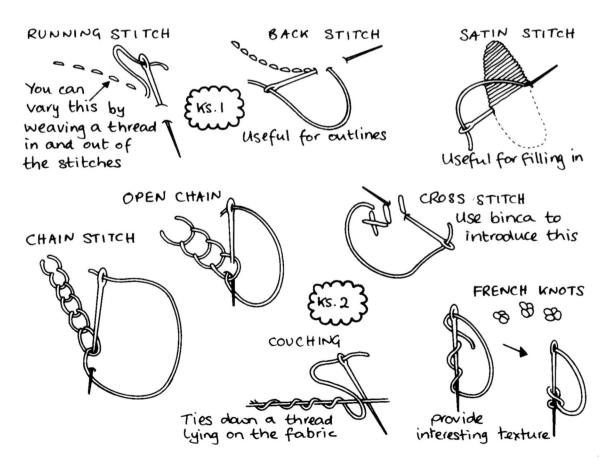

RUNNING STITCH

You can vary this by weaving a thread in and out of the stitches

Ks.1

BACK STITCH

Useful for outlines

SATIN STITCH

Useful for filling in

CHAIN STITCH

OPEN CHAIN

Ks.2

COUCHING

Ties down a thread lying on the fabric

CROSS STITCH
Use binca to introduce this

FRENCH KNOTS

provide interesting texture

Fig.8

Sewing machines

Sewing-machines allow the children to sew faster, and often better. A good sewing-machine can help children to overcome problems of fraying edges and weak seams, and the range of stitches available also will allow decorative effects to be created.

Sewing machines can be used also for embroidery. The children will need to prastise on scraps of material to develop their technique.

The pressure foot which holds the fabric down and the feed dog (the serrated teeth which feeds the fabric under the needle) need to be disengaged so that the fabric can be moved freely about as you sew. A sewing frame is needed to keep the fabric taut. Using a straight stitch and sewing steadily, the fabric can be moved about under the needle to create a design.

Interesting effects can be achieved by tightening the tension of the top thread so that the stitches form loops; this can be used to create textures on the fabric.

Some of the newer computerised sewing machines allow you to alter the speed of the needle, and a slower speed should be used whilst you gain confidence.

Rag dolls

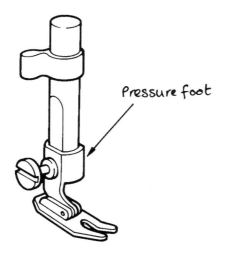

Pressure foot

Feed-dog

Fig.9

4:3 USING FOOD IN DESIGN AND TECHNOLOGY

Children often work with food in the primary school though this experience has not previously been regarded as being part of technology education.

In Part 2 (page 8) we argued that an approach to learning in which the children always follow explicit instructions will not develop design and technology capability. There has to be some decision making by the children. This is true whether the children are working with construction materials, textiles, graphic media or food.

When recipes are used in design and technology work, some aspects of the activity should allow the children to make decisions. For example; when making pizzas, the children might select from a range of toppings for a base prepared to a recipe or provided for them; or select for themselves the ingredients of a fruit salad.

▶ Opportunities for Working with Food

Food is often chosen as a topic in itself, when children look at nutrition, sources of foods, cultural and religious variations and other aspects of the part food plays in our lives. Working with food will be a natural part of such a topic.

Many other topics offer opportunities for working with food. For example, during a project on the Second World War, children might make war-time recipes from the restricted ingredients of the time. As part of a topic on 'the farm', children might make cheese, butter or yoghurt. In this way, they are gaining insights into the different processes for making familiar products.

Sometimes working with food may be organised as a separate activity, outside a topic. This might be related to a celebration, such as bonfire night or a religious festival. Opportunities may be provided for the children to prepare a meal for themselves: breakfast or a lunch, perhaps. When children undertake larger projects, such as planning a meal, the decisions they make might include the combination of dishes, and the recipes to be used, if this is appropriate, to help them to prepare the meal.

As well as learning to prepare and cook food using some of the basic methods characteristic of our own and other cultural traditions, working with food provides contexts for developing awareness of wider, related issues.

▶ Food Packaging and Storage

A visit to a local supermarket can provide an opportunity to focus on the packaging and displaying of food. Younger children can collect empty packages for use in a classroom shop where items may be bought and sold. Other children can investigate the structure and materials of packaging, and design some packaging for food items they have made, such as biscuits.

The nature and quantity of packaging of some foods can be examined to raise important environmental questions about the resources used and their subsequent disposal.

The information on packaging can provide a further line of investigation for older children, supporting work on nutrition. The calorific value, fat, protein, carbohydrate and vitamin content of food, per 100 grams, is usually listed on the wrapping and comparisons can be made about their relative nutritional values.

INGREDIENTS
MAIZE, BROWN SUGAR, PEANUTS, SUGAR, HONEY, SALT, MALT FLAVOURING, NIACIN, IRON, VITAMIN B$_6$, RIBOFLAVIN (B$_2$), THIAMIN (B$_1$), FOLIC ACID, VITAMIN D, VITAMIN B$_{12}$.

NUTRITION INFORMATION Per 100g

ENERGY	1700	kJ
	400	kcal
PROTEIN	7.0	g
CARBOHYDRATE	83	g
of which sugars 35 g		
starch 48 g		
FAT	4.0	g
of which saturates 0.8 g		
SODIUM	0.8	g
FIBRE	1.0	g
VITAMINS:		
NIACIN	16	mg
VITAMIN B$_6$	1.8	mg
RIBOFLAVIN (B$_2$)	1.5	mg
THIAMIN (B$_1$)	1.0	mg
FOLIC ACID	250	µg
VITAMIN D	2.8	µg
VITAMIN B$_{12}$	1.7	µg
IRON	6.7	mg

Fig. 1

Experiences in school can help to guide children towards healthy eating patterns by developing their awareness of the nutritional value of foods.

▶ Preserving Food

Investigation into the storage and preservation of foods can begin from examination of the sell-by dates printed on packages. An awareness can develop of the relationship between the system of preservation and the length of the shelf-life, providing a clear example of the role of technology in our food chain. Some of the processes of preservation are accessible to the children, such as drying herbs and pulses, crystallising fruits, pickling, freezing and jam-making. Processes using high temperatures, such as jam-making, would require close adult supervision.

▶ Fast Food

Eating habits are changing in our society; people are preparing less at home and buying more industrially prepared food.

Pizzas, hamburgers, sandwiches and salads can be made by the children from the basic ingredients, and then costed and compared in price with similar purchased items. They can begin to make judgements about the relative value of purchased food items against home-made items in terms of cost, convenience and taste.

Fast food outlets can provide an interesting starting point for a food project. Thick shakes and hamburgers are often favourites with children, and can be made easily to their own recipes. They can begin to explore the potential of combining alternative ingredients to make burgers, e.g. pulses, nuts, breadcrumbs, cereals and meat substitutes.

▶ Industry Links

A visit, for example, to a bakery in a supermarket, might be a starting point for an industry-based project. Bakeries are a particularly good starting point as it is possible for quite young children at Key Stage 1 to be involved in replicating some of the processes in the classroom. A visit can enable them to observe the production processes, the jobs done and the patterns of organisation.

Using this information, a mini-enterprise scheme can be organised to model it. The children can be assigned jobs, survey the potential market, develop a product range, trial and make their product, cost it, advertise and sell it. With the focus on design and technology, the learning experience will extend into all areas of the curriculum and provide insights into the world of work.

▶ Using Tools

Through their activities children should learn to select and use appropriate tools, as they do in other practical work. Young children may need to learn how to use a knife to spread margarine evenly on bread to make a sandwich. Older children will begin to make comparisons between tools designed to do a similar job. For example, a food processor may chop an onion very quickly, but the time saved can be lost in cleaning the machine.

The evaluation of tools may be made explicit by testing. For example, this can be done by using a fork, a balloon whisk, and an electric mixer to beat egg-whites and comparing the time taken, the effort needed and the cost of each method.

▶ Processes

Within design and technology, activities will need to be structured so that children meet a range of processes used in food preparation. Baking cakes and biscuits is popular and can be valuable but children's experiences should be much wider than this.

The issues we have described should permeate the practical activities which are at the heart of design and technology. As they use and prepare food, children will become familiar with the range of processes available, and the way in which decisions about food are made, taking economic, cultural, aesthetic and nutritional issues into account.

4:4 USING GRAPHIC MEDIA

Graphic media include the 'mark-making' tools like pens, pencils, felt-tips brushes, crayons, charcoal and printing equipment as well as paint, inks, collage and the other 'art' materials children use.

These media are used both during the planning of the work when creating working drawings and in creating an attractive finish, for example, when painting a model or producing fabric designs.

Most of the artwork techniques you teach your children already come into this category. These might include mixing paint to get a particular colour, using different grades of pencils to create a range of tones or dyeing textiles.

▶ *Drawing*

Drawing from observation is much easier than drawing from imagination. Discuss the children's drawings with them as they work, encouraging them to talk it through, describing the shape, the proportions and how the parts link together. Their language and observational skills will be developed and it will help them to make their drawings explicit.

Drawing out their designs before starting to make something helps the children to organise their ideas, to decide shape and scale as well as foresee potential difficulties. For example, the position of a hinge on a moving model must allow movement in the required direction. Observation of the real thing can provide information and insight into these problems.

When drawing in order to create an accurate representation, rather than expressively, it is much easier to work from observation than from memory or imagination.

When drawing the real thing is inappropriate, for example when the children are preparing to make a moving dragon or a model of a medieval castle, they will be helped if they can work from pictures of these things. Several pictures are better than just one because they will provide a range of views or features from which to choose. Sometimes you may want your children to work entirely from their imagination, but using photographs, catalogues, book or magazine illustrations for reference helps when a particular detail, layout, shape or scale is needed.

Just as in handwriting practice where children might use line guides to help their lettering, drawing can be helped in a similar way. Squared paper underlays provide horizontal and vertical guidelines,and can assist in gauging proportion.

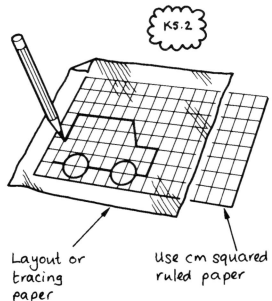

Layout or tracing paper

Use cm squared ruled paper

Fig.1

When the children are going to build a model, encourage them to make a drawing of its most complicated side. For a building this will probably be the front; for a vehicle, the side. If possible, they should make the drawing full size, so that it can be used directly to get the measurements of the different parts. This 'working drawing' can be annotated with comments, descriptions and plans both before and during the work, and will serve as a memo between one session and the next and between one child and another, so good ideas don't get lost or forgotten.

If the model is not too large, a full-scale drawing can be made of its ground plan (the bottom view). If the children use centimetre squared paper, its ruled lines provide a guide for accurate lines and square corners. The squares can represent units of length and the idea of scale can be developed. The model can then be built literally on top of this drawing; this is particularly helpful when using strip wood to make space-frames (such as the 'Jinks' technique).

▶ **Lettering**

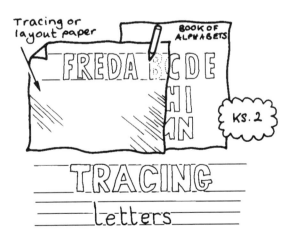

Fig.2

Good design and technology work is sometimes spoiled when wobbly and untidy lettering is added (for example, the lettering on a pop-up greeting card). It is difficult to letter neatly, especially on to a flexible or curved surface and it is better to do the lettering on a separate piece of paper or card, cut it out and stick it into place on the work. This provides an opportunity for you to teach the children some lettering techniques.

Letter shapes can be copied or traced from a book. Catalogues from 'instant lettering' suppliers (Letraset, for example) contain many different and interesting letter styles. These can be copied or traced, if the size is suitable.

The light-weight paper of layout pads is an economical substitute for tracing paper. Soft pencils (B or 2B) grade, are easier and cleaner to erase than harder (HB or H). A soft eraser will be less damaging to the paper surface than a hard one.

Encourage the children to pencil guidelines onto the tracing paper to keep the lettering level. When the message is complete it can be inked in and the pencil marks erased. This method of inking (or felt-tipping) over pencilled drafting is also helpful when preparing drawings.

Plastic lettering stencils also can be used, though the range of letter styles and sizes is limited.

Computer word-processing software such as Folio Plus or Front Page can be used with a printer for producing lettering, decorative borders and other graphic materials.

Older children can use simple masking techniques to get edges on shading with pencil, crayon, felt-tips and colour washes.

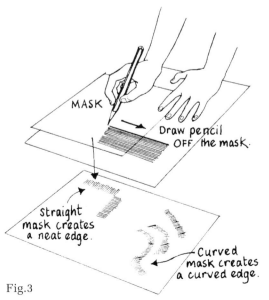

Fig.3

Interest can be added to artwork when images or lettering cut from magazines, catalogues or brochures is incorporated in the children's work. This should be done sparingly so as to enhance rather than replace the child's own artwork.

As well as writing and drawing records of their work, it may be helpful for the children to take a photograph, particularly when a piece of work cannot be kept intact. This is often the case when construction kits are used, or when food is involved.

▶ *Printing Techniques*

When fabrics are used in design and technology work, printing methods may be used to enhance and personalise their appearance. Many of the techniques work equally well on paper.

For example, the paper or fabric to be used for kites can be coloured or patterned by potato or other block print techniques. Marbling, which is done by floating oil-based paint on water onto which paper is laid, produces fascinating swirl patterns. Marbling was common once on book endpapers and examples can be found in many old books. Marbling kits are available from major suppliers.

Thinned down fabric dyes or Brusho-type inks in a diffuser make interesting splatter patterns and stencils can be used to mask out areas or create an image.

Paper and thin card can be appropriately textured by wax-rubbing on a textured surface such as wood or coarse textiles and used on, for example, models of buildings. Sand sprinkled on a thin coat of wet PVA will give a concrete effect.

Graphics techniques of these kinds can be used in a wide range of design and technology activities. As well as finding out about them from reference books, the children can invent their own techniques through varying those they know and experimenting to make particular effects for a piece of work.

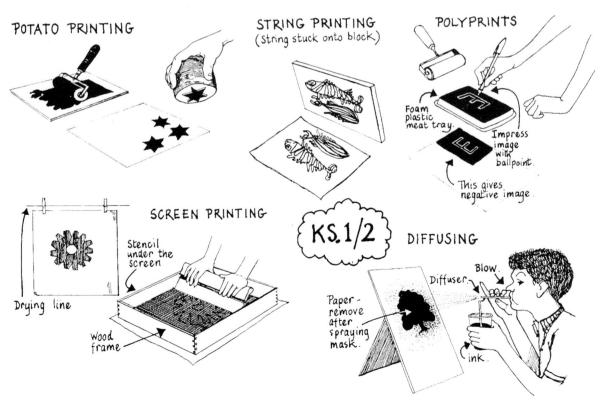

Fig. 4

4:5 MOVING ALONG

Wheels play a significant part in our society and it is not surprising that they encompass many important technological concepts.

The invention of the wheel marks a milestone in human creativity, and we recognise this in expressions like "there's no point in re-inventing the wheel", i.e. no point in doing again something that's already been done satisfactorily. However, as children quickly discover, wheels are not much use without axles, and it helps the children avoid unnecessary difficulties if wheels and axles are always considered together. The wheel is the visible part of the partnership and it's easy to see what it is doing as it rolls along.

Fixing wheels and axles to model vehicles is a common starting point in technology for teachers and children. The techniques they learn can be used wherever wheels and axles occur. Not all wheels are used to transport things over the ground; pulleys and gearwheels and the winder that lifts the bucket from the well are all members of the same large and widespread family.

Just how the wheels, the axles and the structure can all be connected together is not immediately obvious, and there is a sort of 'axle readiness', a degree of experience, that has to be reached before the whole thing is understood clearly. If the wheels are fixed to the axles and the axles are fixed to the vehicle body, the wheels won't be able to turn and the vehicle won't roll along.

There are two ways of mounting wheels and axles. These are:

- the axle is fixed to the structure and the wheels are free to spin on the axle;

- the wheels are fixed to the axle, and the axle is free to turn in its guides.

If you can make a collection of wheeled toys, small machines and models, you should find both kinds for the children to examine.

Model with axle fixed and wheels free to turn

Model with wheels fixed and axle free to turn

▶ Fixing Axles

At Key Stage 1, children can become familiar with the ways in which wheels and axles function together through the use of construction kits.

When making box models of vehicles, children will often fit notional wheels by painting circles or by gluing circular cheese boxes onto the wheel positions. An effective way to develop this is to encourage them to fit wheels that turn.

A good way to start is to use a paper fastener, pushed through the middle of each cheese box and into the side of the vehicle body, to provide an axle on which the wheel can turn. The bottoms of the wheels will have to be brought below the bottom of the body or the wheels won't touch the ground. Finding out the right positions for the wheels and their centres can provide an opportunity to investigate the properties of circles.

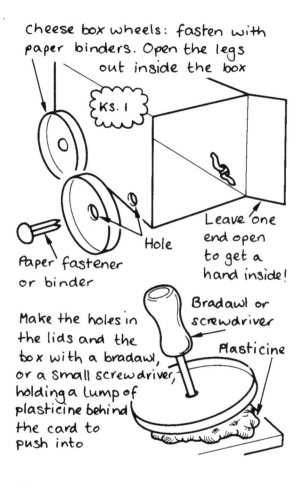

Fig.1

There are many ways of fixing non-turning axles to a box including using Sellotape, gluing them or pushing them through tight holes in the body. With fixed axles, the wheels have to be fitted to the axle loosely enough to turn but not so loosely that they wobble too much. It is easiest here to use thick wheels, so that there is a wide bearing surface; even a quite loose-fitting wheel will stand up straight if wide enough.

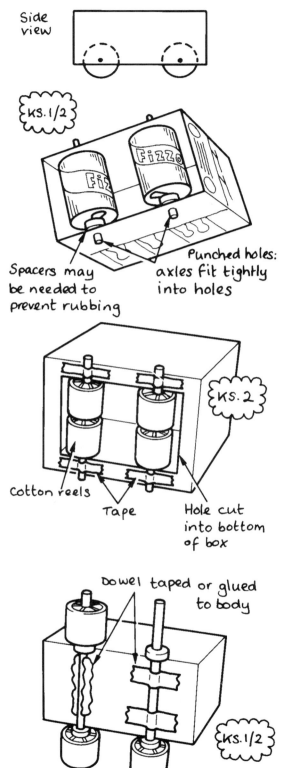

Fig.2

▶ Axles Turning Freely in an Axle Bearer

The problem that has to be solved is how to fix the axle to the vehicle body tightly enough not to fall off but loosely enough to allow it to turn.

When a box is used to form the vehicle's body the children may decide to make holes in the card sides of the vehicle body for the axle to pass through, and this works if the holes are not left too furry (creating more frictional resistance). If the holes are too big, pieces of card, with holes punched in them, can be glued on top to align the axle more accurately. It is difficult to make sure the axles are parallel using this method.

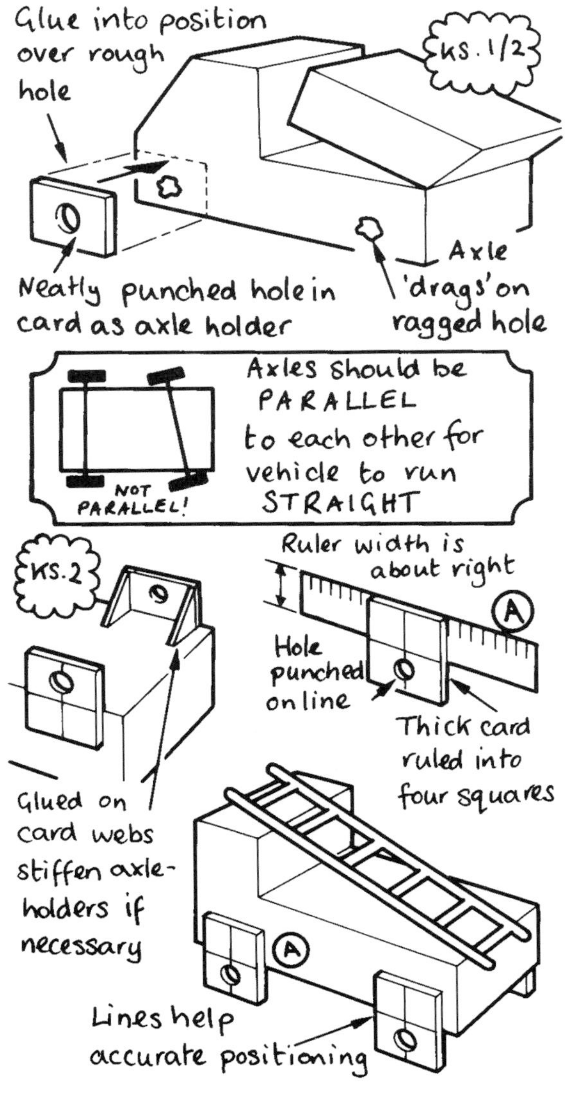

An alternative method is for the axle to be supported in a tube fixed to the underside of the box. The tube, which might be a jumbo art straw or the barrel of a pen, must be large enough for the axle to turn freely inside it.

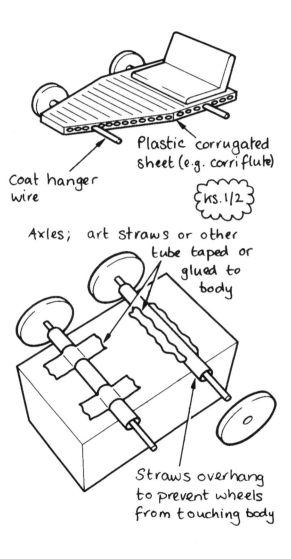

Coat hanger wire

Plastic corrugated sheet (e.g. corriflute)

ᏇKS.1/2᠁

Axles; art straws or other tube taped or glued to body

Straws overhang to prevent wheels from touching body

Fig.4

Glue into position over rough hole

ᏇKS.1/2᠁

Neatly punched hole in card as axle holder

Axle 'drags' on ragged hole

Axles should be PARALLEL to each other for vehicle to run STRAIGHT

NOT PARALLEL!

ᏇKS.2᠁

Glued on card webs stiffen axle-holders if necessary

Ruler width is about right

Hole punched on line

Thick card ruled into four squares

Ⓐ

Lines help accurate positioning

Fig.3

If the children are working with wood, electrical cable clips can be used as axle bearings. You might find that the nails that accompany the clips are too large for the small sections of wood that the children are likely to be using. Replace them with panel pins; 15 mm panel pins would be suitable for 8 mm wood.

67

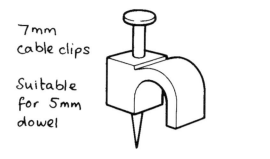

7mm cable clips

Suitable for 5mm dowel

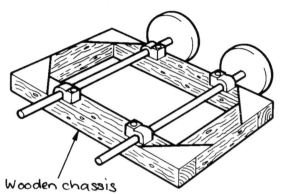

Wooden chassis
At key stage 1, it might be more appropriate for the children to use a solid piece of wood instead of constructing a frame

Fig.5

You may provide, for the children's use, wooden dowel for axles and plywood wheels which are pre-drilled to fit tightly onto the dowel. The wheels and the axle turn together and this avoids the problem of preventing the wheels from wobbling or even falling off their axle.

Plywood wheels are usually supplied pre-drilled to push-fit onto 5 mm dowel. If the fit is too tight, don't enlarge the hole or the wheel will wobble. Instead, turn the end of the dowel just once in a pencil sharpener to bevel the end. This makes it easier to start it into the hole.

If the wheel is too loose add a single thickness of Sellotape (or more if necessary) around the end of the axle to increase its diameter. This is a neater method than gluing and allows you to remove the wheel if need be.

Children will begin by using familiar materials to solve new problems, for example, by twisting loops in pipe-cleaners as axle-guides, and pushing axles through lumps of Blu-Tak pressed on to the base of the vehicle. Being soft, these create a lot of friction and allow too much loose movement to be very effective, but they are not 'wrong'. Technological answers are not right or wrong; only more or less effective. The appropriateness of the solution is relative to the child's stage of development and previous experience, and this needs to be considered before more sophisticated ideas are introduced. Don't be tempted to provide your children always with a complete solution. It is more helpful to discuss with the children what they think the characteristics of an axle bearer are (such as having a low-friction surface, being able to hold the axle without constraining it, being of reasonable size, being able to be fixed rigidly to the vehicle body, etc) and let them see what might do the job. Quite often they will suggest something you hadn't thought of, and it might work. It is essential for the children to go through the process of deciding, through thought, discussion, trial and error, just what the problem is.

Whichever method of mounting wheels and axles is used, it is good practice to try spinning the wheels to see if they turn freely. Sometimes the friction in the bearing surfaces can be reduced by lubrication with candle wax or furniture polish. Hard waxes work better than soft waxes on wood and other absorbent materials. Make sure that the bearing surfaces don't get painted or this will increase enormously the friction between them.

4:6 ELECTRICAL CIRCUITS

The overlap between science and technology is especially close when children are working with electricity. The knowledge defined by the science programmes of study will be encompassed by children's design and technology activities, and need not be approached in isolation.

At Key Stages 1 and 2, children must have opportunities to investigate batteries, wires, lights and buzzers, to see how they connect together and work, and to investigate the conductivity and insulation properties of common materials. All this exploration is essential and children love to do it.

From this point, real working circuits can be built: a child modelling a lighthouse can add realism with a lamp that lights up; a crane which previously operated manually may be motorised. Rather than setting up special electricity projects, an electrification programme can run through other work where appropriate, enhancing that work and putting learning about electricity in a real context.

Add realism to a model lighthouse with a lamp that lights

▶ Batteries

Much failure, frustration and expense can be avoided if you make sure that the components you supply to the children are all compatible with one another. Decide which batteries you are going to supply and match all your components to the same voltage. If you provide 6-volt batteries and 1.5-volt bulbs, when the children make a circuit the bulbs will blow immediately; 6-volt bulbs will hardly light at all if connected to a 1.5-volt battery.

It doesn't really matter which voltage you standardise upon, so long as it is very low; we use 1.5 volts because the batteries are at the cheaper end of the range, are easily available and are small enough to incorporate discretely into models.

Problems will arise during this process, of course, and this section is concerned with avoiding the sort of difficulties that lead to frustration and confusion, and exploiting those difficulties whose solutions lead to understanding.

▶ Rechargeable Batteries

Rechargeable batteries are more expensive to buy but can be re-used many times so are good value for money. But, there are two points to note:

- if the positive end of the battery is accidently connected to the negative end without any lamp, buzzer or other working part in between (this is called a short-circuit) the battery can give up all of its stored energy rapidly. The connecting wire can become quite hot, perhaps even dangerously so, and many teachers, and some LEAs, have been dissuaded from using them. This does not happen with a conventional battery, which will simply die slowly and quietly,
- some rechargeable batteries supply not 1.5 volts, as does a conventional battery, but 1.2 volts, and whilst 1.5-volt components will work on this, they are slightly underpowered.

▶ Power Supply Units

Instead of batteries, you can use power supply units (PSUs) which plug into the mains and give out battery-like power (2-12 volts DC). If you have a computer control interface box, it may have a built-in PSU which you can use in non-computerised circuits. The main advantage of a PSU is that once you have one you never need to buy a battery again. They cost almost nothing to run but they are expensive to buy. You can't build them easily into models, unless you trail wires to the plug, and the children can't take home a working model unless they first convert it to battery power.

▶ Making Connections to the Battery

The best way to obtain a good and reliable connection between the wires in a circuit and the battery is to use a battery box. Simply holding the wires to the terminals is appropriate only for investigations. Once the circuit is supposed to do something other than demonstrate itself, no-one will be satisfied with having to hold the wires on to the battery. Some books recommend sticking wires on to batteries with Sellotape or Blu-Tak, or trapping the wires under rubber bands, but these are not very secure; movement and vibration in the model will soon cause the poor connection at the battery to fail. All this can be avoided easily by using battery boxes. These are open-topped plastic boxes into which batteries fit snugly against terminals with wires trailing out. They cost very little (when ordering, specify the size of the battery it will contain), or they can be made using a film cannister, two paper fasteners or drawing pins, and two pieces of connector block.

▶ Wire

As far as safety is concerned, almost any kind of wire can be used in the low-powered circuits your children will build, though thick or stiff wire like house wiring cable will be difficult for them to handle. If you have a choice, multi-strand wire is the best type for school use, being more flexible than single-strand wire and less likely to break. We use 7/0.2 wire (7 strands, 0.2 sq mm cross-sectional area). A good source of high quality wire is telephone cable offcuts; strip off the cream sleeve to reveal four brightly-coloured wires.

▶ Joining Wires

The usual, quick way of joining wires in a circuit is to twist them together. This is not a good method. Each twist provides another potential break in the circuit, and there can be quite a lot of them, for example, in a headlight circuit on a model vehicle. The chances of a failure are high. Connector blocks, in which the wires are actually screwed down, overcome this problem.

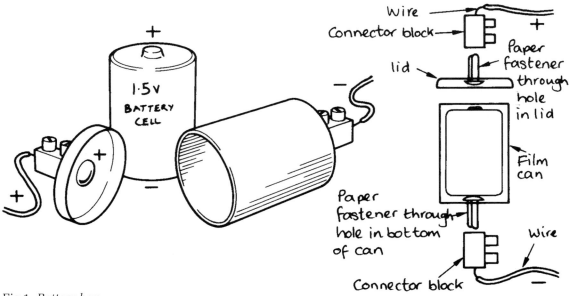

Fig.1 *Battery box*

▶ Plastic Connector Strip

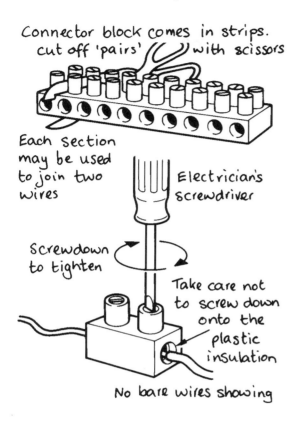

Connector block comes in strips. cut off 'pairs' with scissors

Each section may be used to join two wires

Electrician's screwdriver

Screwdown to tighten

Take care not to screw down onto the plastic insulation

No bare wires showing

Fig.2 *Using a connector block*

Whatever battery voltage you decide upon, be sure all other components are designed to run on or close to that voltage. Most other useful components are listed below.

▶ Bulbs and Bulb Holders

Bulbs come in two main types of fittings: **bayonet**, similar to the fitting of the normal household lightbulb, and **screw** type. The bulbs and the bulb holders have to match. It is not always easy to obtain bulb holders for the bayonet type, so you will find it best to standardise on screw fittings, of which the small ones are called MES (Miniature Edison Screw) bulbs. If you intend using a 1.5-volt battery then you will require 1.25 or 1.5-volt bulbs. A difference of half a volt between the bulb and the battery will not cause any problems.

There are two main types of bulb holder available: the MES **batton** holder and a smaller moulded **nylon clip-on** MES bulb holder.

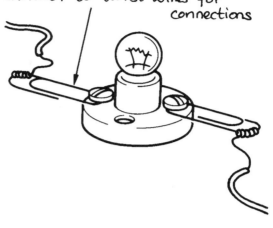

Paper clips trapped under screws make it easier for young children to twist wires for connections

Fig.3 *MES batton holder*

The batton holder which has a flat base with holes to screw it down to a batton (hence the name) is the type once commonly used in schools. Made out of bakelite-type plastic, connections are made by two screw fittings. Children often remove the screws whereupon the holder falls to pieces and it is a fiddly task to put it all back together again. It requires a level of manual dexterity to make the connection at the little screws, and young children sometimes find this difficult.

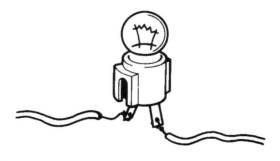

Fig.4 *Nylon clip-on holder*

The smaller, cheaper nylon clip-on bulb holder with two metal tags to which connections are made is less bulky and easier to build into models, though care must be taken to ensure that the bulb is screwed down fully.

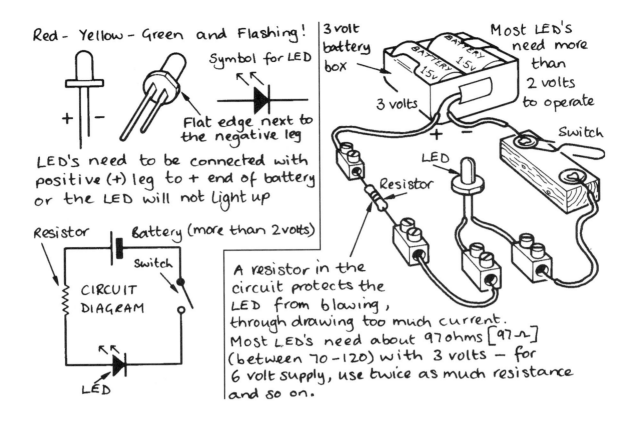

Red - Yellow - Green and Flashing!

Symbol for LED

Flat edge next to the negative leg

LED's need to be connected with positive (+) leg to + end of battery or the LED will not light up

Resistor   Battery (more than 2 volts)

Switch

CIRCUIT DIAGRAM

LED

3 volt battery box

3 volts

Most LED's need more than 2 volts to operate

Switch

LED

Resistor

A resistor in the circuit protects the LED from blowing, through drawing too much current. Most LED's need about 97 ohms [97-Ω] (between 70-120) with 3 volts — for 6 volt supply, use twice as much resistance and so on.

Fig.5 *Working with LEDs*

▶ LEDs

LEDs (Light Emitting Diodes) are small, glowing bulb-like indicator lights now common on all kinds of electronic equipment. There are three red ones on the BBC computer keyboard, for example. You can buy them in red, yellow or green. Unlike bulbs, they glow rather than shine and they give out much less heat. They are cheaper to buy than bulbs, they don't need a holder and they are small enough to fit easily into models. They have to be connected with the positive leg to the battery positive (unlike bulbs, which work either way round) but if incorrectly connected won't be harmed; they just won't light up. A diode is a kind of one-way valve for electrical current flow and there are certain sorts of diodes which don't glow, for other electronic purposes.

LEDs appear brightest when viewed end-on, rather than from the side, so it's best to mount them by making a hole and pushing the head of the LED through from the back, so that just the top is visible. You even can get flashing diodes, though as yet these are not cheap.

▶ Motors

Most motors will run on a range of voltages, so, for example, a six-volt motor will run on 1.5 volts, but more slowly and less effectively than it would at the correct voltage. Too high a voltage will make it run very fast though not for very long because it will die of overheating.

▶ Buzzers

There isn't a great variety of buzzers nor are there many inexpensive ones available. Three-volt buzzers will work on 1.5-volts, but with less volume (this may be preferable!). Like the LEDs, buzzers will have to be connected by positive lead to the battery positive, and similarly won't be harmed if wrongly polarised. You can use this phenomenon to sound a reversing alarm on a motorised model vehicle (see motors section).

▶ Switches

When children are learning to use electricity, it is well worth encouraging them to make their own switches so that they have a clear idea of what happens when a switch is operated. The drawings here show how some switches can be made. Once they are familiar with the simpler switches, bought switches may be introduced, though their use will probably have to be limited due to the costs involved.

Switches you will find useful are:
- **toggle** switches. These stay *on* or *off* when you have operated them and are the most common of all electrical control devices. They have two connection tags. The light switch in a room is an example of this kind of switch. This is the easiest kind of switch for children to make themselves;
- **press** (or push) switches. These are like door bell switches. They only work while you press them.They have two connection tags.

To save confusion, switches are not normally described as being *off* or *on*, but *open* or *closed* respectively.

Most push switches, like the door-bell switch, are 'normally open' (n/o), that is, not *on* until you press it. But, you can get 'normally closed' (n/c) switches which are *on* (closed) until you press them when they go *off* (open). The fridge light works like this.

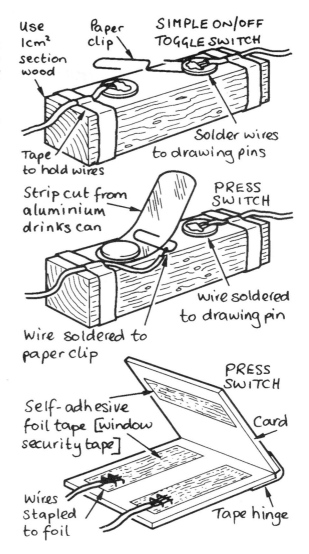

Fig.6 *Toggle and press switches*

NORMALLY-CLOSED SWITCH

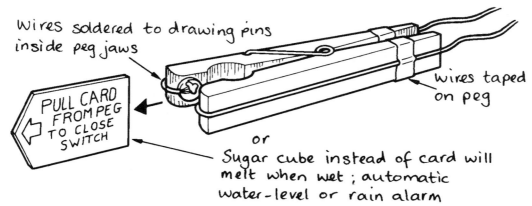

Fig.7 *Normally-closed switch*

- **reed** switches. These are operated by a magnet. The switch is made from two separate pieces of metal which are enclosed in a glass tube. When a magnet is brought near, the two pieces of metal move together and the switch closes (switches *on*). When the magnet is removed the switch opens again.

- **micro** switches. These are sensitive press switches which have three or four terminals and can be wired in several different ways.

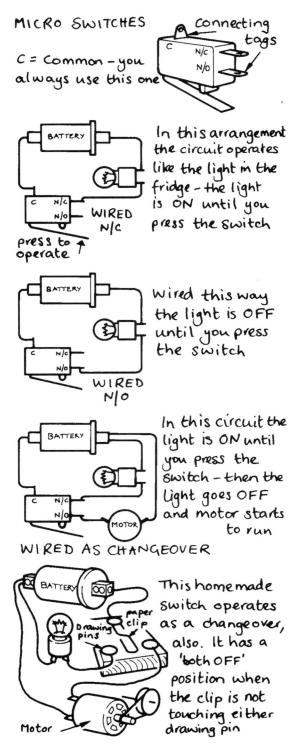

MICRO SWITCHES — Connecting tags

C = Common - you always use this one

In this arrangement the circuit operates like the light in the fridge - the light is ON until you press the switch

WIRED N/C — press to operate ↑

Wired this way the light is OFF until you press the switch

WIRED N/O

In this circuit the light is ON until you press the switch - then the light goes OFF and motor starts to run

WIRED AS CHANGEOVER

This homemade switch operates as a changeover, also. It has a 'both OFF' position when the clip is not touching either drawing pin

Fig.9 *Micro switches*

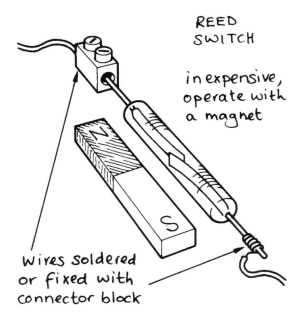

REED SWITCH

inexpensive, operate with a magnet

Wires soldered or fixed with connector block

Fig.7 *Reed switch*

Reed switches are interesting and useful because they operate remotely; the magnet doesn't have to physically touch the switch, just pass close by.

Enclosing the reeds in the glass tube excludes oxygen from the contact, reducing the minute burning that takes place each time the switch operates. This makes them very long-lasting and reliable and millions of them were used in telephone exchanges before the invention of electronic switches (in which no parts move at all).

Another important use is in places where explosive gases might be present, such as in mines. The glass envelope prevents the spark setting off the gas.

- **motor reversing** switches. Older children can make a switch which will reverse a motor by changing the polarity of the battery connections.

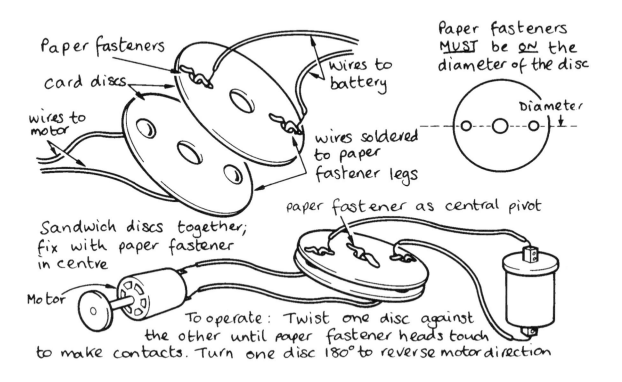

Fig.10 *Making a motor-reversing switch*

There are many more kinds of switches, some of quite amazing subtlety, but those listed here should do just about everything your children will want. Many examples of switches can be found in houses, cars, domestic equipment and toys and the children may be able to identify them by their operation.

The main technological concern with electricity is with the idea of control, and in practice this usually means looking at switches of various kinds. As well as hand-operated (fridge) and door-operated (car) switches, children may be able to spot switches operated by heat (water heater), a time-clock (central heating), light (street lights), sound (burglar alarm), and many other kinds of signal. This will also provide a good opportunity to emphasise the potential dangers of mains electricity, and the importance of treating it with the utmost respect and caution.

▶ *Kits*

Instead of children building circuits from separate components, it is possible for them to work with one of the many attractive kits available. Some science schemes require specific kits which are designed for stand-alone investigations initiated through workcards. Apart from their cost, the main disadvantage of kits is their inevitable tendency to treat electricity as something to be studied and learned, not something to be used to achieve a purpose. Most kits cannot, except with considerable ingenuity, be incorporated into children's models. Even if they can, an expensive kit is then tied up in one model leaving the kit incomplete and probably unusable. Also, the electrical parts can't go home with the model. It is not difficult, and much cheaper, for you to assemble your own kit of components which can be used both for investigations and applications.

▶ Circuits

At the lower end of Key Stage 1, a first introduction to electrical circuits may come through children using a circuit which you have provided for them. The children may spend some time experimenting with the equipment and this period of investigation can be used to introduce the idea of conductors and insulators.

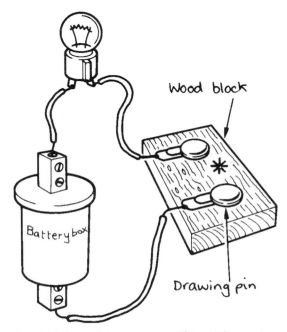

✳ **Bridge the gap with different materials to find which will conduct electricity**

Fig.11 *Completing a simple circuit*

The first circuit the children build, will probably consist of simply a battery and a bulb connected with wires. Children will be familiar with the idea of a switch being used to turn a light on and off and this idea will be developed when they make switches from easily available materials. This allows them to see and understand that a switch introduces a break into the circuit preventing the current from flowing. Some ideas for making switches have been shown but it is important that children are encouraged to develop and use their own ideas as they gain experience.

▶ Drawing Circuits

Although drawing electrical circuit diagrams is not specifically mentioned until Level 5 it is worth encouraging the children to record the circuits they have built from the very beginning. Key Stage 1 children might draw the circuit as it is set out before them; older children may use symbols to represent the components (either conventional or of their own choice). As the children gain experience and their circuits become more complex, the need to plan in advance will become apparent. The circuit plan will also be useful for checking the wiring when trouble-shooting.

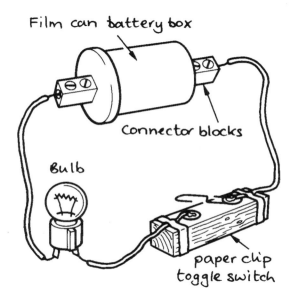

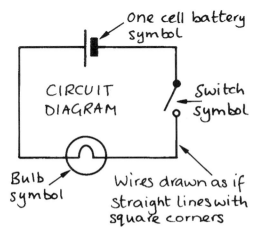

Fig.12 *Drawing a simple circuit*

▶ Series and Parallel Circuits

Next come circuits with more than one component, a circuit which lights two lights, for example. If you let the children try to work this out for themselves they will find that there are two ways of doing this; one in which the two lights are in 'series' and one where they are in 'parallel'.

These two examples allow children to observe the effects of varying the flow of electricity in a circuit.

Let us look at a situation where the problem of parallel and series circuits might arise, e.g. headlights on a vehicle. This provides an ideal opportunity for children to investigate the differences between these two types of circuit.

Shared between the two lamps, each will receive 1.5 V and so will work at their proper brightness. This solution, however, conflicts with the general good practice of keeping the components' values matched, e.g. 1.5 V battery with 1.5 V bulbs.

A better and more realistic solution is a parallel circuit where the components work independently of each other, and operate at their optimum efficiency.

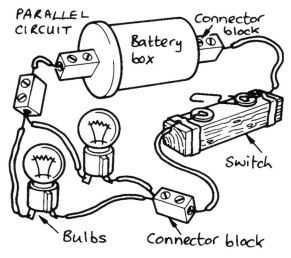

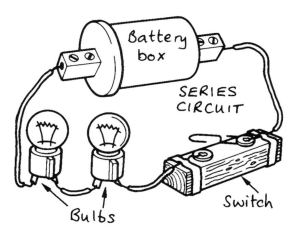

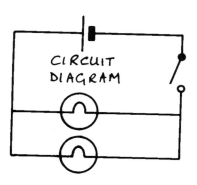

Fig.14 *A parallel circuit*

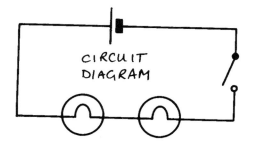

Fig.13 *A series circuit*

If the children's first solution is a series circuit the lights will be insufficiently bright. One solution would be to add another battery, end-on with the first (i.e. in series) to provide 3 V.

The children can investigate the effects of placing the switch in different places in the circuit. Although we have shown lights in these circuits, the same circuits will operate other components such as a buzzer or a motor.

▶ Flashing Lights

Sometimes your children will want a light to flash on and off, not just stay on permanently, for example, in a lighthouse or on a police car or fire engine. There are lots of ways of achieving this besides operating the switch yourself. The method most accessible to children is to use a reed switch and magnets. When the magnet passes close to the reed, it will switch on.

Continuous flashing can be achieved by fixing the magnet onto a rotating surface so that with each turn the magnet operates the reed switch. So, a magnet fixed onto a vehicle's wheel will operate a reed mounted next to the wheel to get one flash on and off per rotation as the vehicle rolls along. More than one magnet will give a different pattern of flashes, and two magnets mounted close together will give a long flash.

▶ Using Motors

Ways of using electric motors are described in Part 4:7. When you connect a motor to a battery, the motor spindle will spin rapidly. Change the polarity of the battery (turn the battery end to end) and the motor will turn in the opposite direction. By turning the battery connections around you can make a vehicle run forwards and backwards, or make a crane lift and lower.

For most primary school uses, turning the battery around will give sufficient motor control. It is possible to buy and wire up a reversing switch or to make one which will demonstrate more clearly just how the polarity is reversed (see motor reversing switches on page 75).

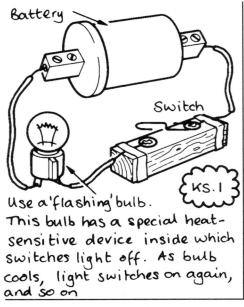

Use a 'flashing' bulb. This bulb has a special heat-sensitive device inside which switches light off. As bulb cools, light switches on again, and so on

KS.1

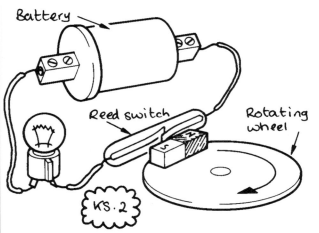

The light switches on when magnet on rotating wheel passes close to reed switch

KS.2

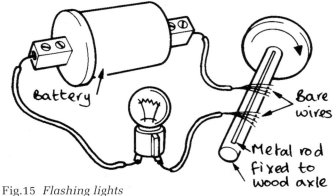

The light switches on as both bare wires touch metal rod on rotating axle.
Metal rod conducts and completes the circuit

KS.2

Fig.15 *Flashing lights*

▶ Fault-finding

It is always pleasing when a circuit works first time but, paradoxically, fault-finding and correcting is the most effective way to develop the capability to use electricity. It is important that the children develop a logical and methodical approach to fault-finding, seeing it as an interesting challenge.

1. **Look**. Quite often you can solve the problem simply by looking at the circuit when you realise you've forgotten to connect up the battery, for example, or left out one of the wires.
2. **Check connections**. Gently tug the wires to make sure they are not loose. Check connector blocks to make sure the plastic insulation is not trapped under the screws.
3. **Check components**. Test individual components, including the battery, by substituting other components known to work. it is essential that this is done one component at at time, and this is where a methodical approach really pays off.
4. **Check the circuit**. Make sure that the circuit itself is correct. Follow each wire in turn, checking that it starts and finishes where it ought to. It often helps here to talk it through out loud.

The whole fault-finding process is very much more effective when two people are working on it together.

▶ Soldering

The problems with poor connections can be reduced substantially by providing the children with bulb holders and motors with short (10 cm) leads pre-soldered to the tags. Soldering is an easy skill to master once you have been taught how to do it. When the children make their own switches it will be useful to give them short leads soldered to drawing pins and paper fasteners. Until someone invents a conducting glue, soldering is the most reliable, quickest and cheapest way of making electrical connections.

Don't try soldering wires directly to batteries; the large mass of the battery makes it difficult to form a reliable joint. If soldering is out of the question it is possible to attach connector blocks to the terminals of bulb holders and motors. You may need some heavier duty connector strip to do this.

4:7 USING ENERGY

Energy is a central technological concept and powering models which they have made provides children with an opportunity to use a wide variety of energy sources. In this way, they are able to develop an awareness of how energy can be collected, stored and controlled so that a useful task is performed. There are close links with science here, and opportunities to approach the statements of attainment through practical activities.

Problems of controlling friction will arise when children are using energy sources to power their models. The quality of their model making can cause difficulties, for example, through rough finishes or paint on the axles. Sometimes unsuitable materials are to blame, e.g. using pipe-cleaners for axle bearers (see Part 4:5). This would be a good time to stand back from the task to investigate the properties of different materials for a particular use.

Not all power sources are used to drive axles, of course, but many of them do so at some stage in the process of converting one type of energy or motion to another. This is mainly because rotary motion (a shaft turning) stays conveniently in the same place, unlike linear motion which moves along (a wind mill converts the wind's linear motion to rotary motion to drive the mill-stones). Consequently, most machines and devices use axles of some kind and these are often the source of unwanted friction (though not all friction is unwanted; brakes depend on the use of friction).

The children's models can provide examples of devices which collect, store, convert and use energy. The difficulties inherent in these operations can often be more easily seen in a small working model than in commercial machinery. All working models use energy and many of the ideas discussed below are illustrated and developed in Part 3.

The main energy sources suitable for powering children's models include:
• muscles;
• gravity;
• wind;
• solar;
• strain;
• electricity.

▶ Muscles

Until recently we had to rely on our own strength, or that of animals, to do work. Using a horse or an ox to pull something along was, of course, much easier than doing it oneself. Before the invention of the steam engine, animal-driven machinery was commonly used to pump the water from deep coal and tin mines; sometimes children were used to bucket the water up.

A model of a horse-powered wind gin

Children's models which work by pushing, pulling or hand-winding are using muscle power. Even models which eventually are to use some other power source should be tested first by hand. Problems of friction or poor alignment of parts which will affect performance should be corrected at this stage.

▶ Gravity

A next logical step, for models which roll along, is to use the force of gravity to pull them down a slope when children can investigate the effects of changing the angle of the slope. The force of gravity also can be used, for example, to pull models up a slope or to rotate a shaft.

Fig.1 *Working with the force of gravity*

Gravity acting on counterweights can be used to assist another form of power. This is very common in liftshafts and in level crossing barriers.

Gliders, flying seeds and birds all use the force of gravity, combined often with the wind and uplifting thermal currents, to travel (see Part 3).

Water flowing downhill due to gravity is an important source of power, used today in hydroelectric power stations. Historically, the water-powered corn mill was a feature of many early settlements. These mills used a similar arrangement of gears to those in the windmill to convert the motion of the horizontal shaft turned by the water wheel, to the vertical shaft and the stones.

Bevel gears in a watermill

Ironworkers used water-powered bellows to ensure a good flow of air to the coals in the forge in order to maintain the fierce heat necessary to work the iron.

Much of the early steel industry of Sheffield was based around the hundreds of tiny mills along the valleys in the city, where water power was used to turn the machinery which hammered and ground the implements manufactured there. The machinery in these mills was driven by leather belts connected to the main water-driven shaft.

In the 18th century, water power changed spinning and weaving from a home-based cottage industry to a factory-based concern.

Children's models which come in contact with water (for example, watermills, paddles and boats) need to be water-resistant. There are two approaches to achieving this: waterproof materials can be used or models can be made waterproof after they are complete. Plastics may be joined with hot glue or insulating tape (not Sellotape). Models can be varnished or painted with gloss paint, though these take time to dry and can be messy. The children could investigate these and other methods and materials to make an informed choice.

▶ Wind

The use of wind as a power source is longstanding. The Egyptians used sailing boats more than 5000 years ago. Before this, it is thought that boats relied on muscle power. Later, the energy of wind was harnessed to drive machinery. The energy collectors, usually some form of sails attached to the shaft of an electricity generator, were relatively simple machines.

Wind power still plays an important role in societies whose technology is not very advanced. Relying as it does on a free, inexhaustible source of energy, wind power makes an important contribution to the world economy and in future may become important in our own society once more as energy costs increase and environmental issues become more pressing.

Children's models can capture energy from the wind with sails on windmills, boats and land yachts and with kites.

▶ Solar

The movement of the wind is caused by the sun heating the planet unevenly, so the wind is an effect of solar energy. Using solar energy directly to drive models is more difficult without the use of electronic devices to convert light to electricity (photo-cells). These are already available and rapidly becoming cheaper. Soon, they will be as useful as batteries to drive electrical circuits.

▶ Strain

Energy can be stored by deforming some flexible material; the energy is recovered when the material is allowed to revert to its former shape. This idea is used in bows, spring-boards, clocksprings, clothes pegs, paper clips and catapults. Using the stretch of an elastic band to power something is a familiar idea and you may have used it to fire pieces of paper across a classroom. Energy stored in this form is called strain energy.

In medieval times strain energy was used to power siege weapons. Sometimes, the energy was stored in the structure itself. Strong ropes supporting the firing arm were twisted and the wooden structure bent, storing enough energy to fire the missile (other designs used gravity but these were not so effective).

Models of seige weapons which use strain energy

It may seem that strain energy would be one of the easier ways for children to power their models but this is not usually the case. The amount of strain energy that an ordinary elastic band can store is small (underwater spearfishermen use very large, thick rubber bands to fire their spears). In addition, the release of energy can be very rapid; ideal for firing spears but difficult to control.

One of the most successful ways for young children to use strain energy is the 'cotton reel crawler' idea and there are many variations of this. Here, an elastic band is threaded through a cylinder, anchored at one end and looped over a rod at the other. The cylinder does not have to be a cotton reel; a drinks can, drinks bottle, custard tin or other kind of cardboard tube will do.

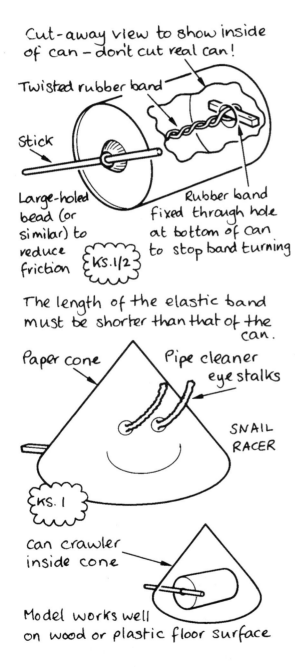

Fig.2 *Making a cotton-reel crawler*

▶ Electricity

One advantage of using power from the wind or water is the absence of fuel costs; but what happens during very calm weather or when there is a drought? The invention of the steam engine helped to solve that problem. The steam engine, and then the internal combustion engine quickly replaced much of the wind-powered and water-powered machinery.

Today in the developed world, we have diversified our power sources to such an extent that calms and droughts aren't everyday energy worries. Those who use wind power can use batteries or generators for back-up when the wind fails. Most of us don't even think about where our power comes from; in our homes we are so reliant on electrical appliances, we seldom give the source of that electricity a thought until there is a power cut.

During discussions about energy provision it is vital that children come to appreciate the associated environmental issues. These include the limited supply of fossil fuels and the harmful effects their use is having on the earth's atmosphere, and nuclear energy with the problems of disposal of radioactive waste. These are complex issues but are often mentioned on TV and radio programmes, in the press and in children's literature, and may be familiar ideas to your children.

▶ Using Electricity

Just as electrical energy is easily accessible in the home, it is accessible also to children in their projects. Unlike wind and water power, collecting the energy is not a problem since batteries provide the power; generating electricity is more complex than most primary age children might manage.

In Part 4:6, we discussed electrical power sources and the wiring up an electric motor in a circuit. Fitting motors to models and using their energy to do some useful work raises a variety of important technological ideas.

When you make a motor circuit you will find that the motor shaft rotates very rapidly; probably too rapidly to be used directly. The actual speed of the motor depends on a number of factors, but if the voltage of the motor is matched by the battery it may rotate faster than 4000 revolutions per minute (rpm). This can be reduced by using a smaller battery, but this will also have the effect of reducing the turning force. This turning force is called 'torque'. Try grasping the motor shaft between your fingers and notice how much easier it is to stop it when you use the smaller battery. Conversely, if you increase the voltage the motor will go faster and eventually, if you exceed the makers' recommended voltage by too much, the motor will overheat and burn out.

These small, low-cost motors tend to give high speed and low torque and unless you can use some means of increasing their torque they are not very useful. The easiest way of doing this is to use some form of belt drive.

On a sewing machine, a rubber belt takes the drive from the motor shaft around the larger pulley wheel. The sewing mechanism is driven more slowly but with more force than if it was connected directly to the motor.

Pulley mechanisms and gear boxes convert fast, weak motion into slow, forceful motion (as in the sewing machine) and vice-versa. They trade between speed and torque, the rate of exchange depending on the ratio of the gears or pulley diameters. Their other main job is to connect the source of power (muscle power, electric motor, windmill sail-shaft, etc) to some device that does a useful task, e.g. pump water, grind corn, turn road-wheels, raise and lower car windows, beat eggs.

If the children are using a motor on their model they will, almost always, have to slow it down and make it more forceful, for example, when motorising a vehicle.

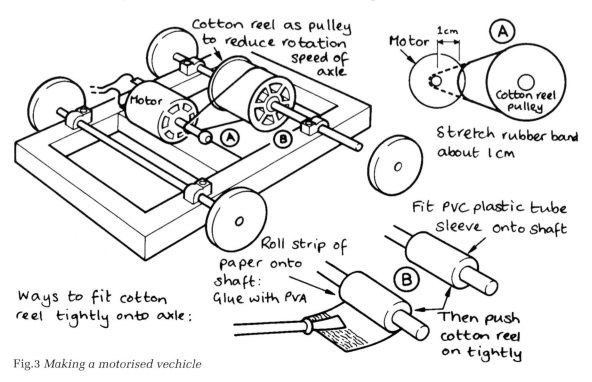

Fig.3 *Making a motorised vechicle*

You can see that the best way is by performing the same task as that on the sewing machine. By connecting the motor shaft to an axle by means of a belt (an elastic band) over a pulley, the speed of the second axle will be reduced to a useful speed, and the increased power will allow the stationary vehicle to move forward.

In using a pulley, you will have effectively increased the diameter of the axle so that for one turn of the motor shaft the axle will only rotate a small amount. It will take many turns of the motor shaft to make the axle complete one turn.

The reduction in speed can be calculated easily by estimating or measuring the diameters of the motor shaft and pulley. This is much easier to understand when you can see it: look at the diagram of the drinks can below. The axle with the large pulley turns appreciably slower than the motor shaft.

In this instance, the pulley axle is rotating 10 times slower than the motor because the pulley is 10 times bigger, it also will have 10 times more torque.

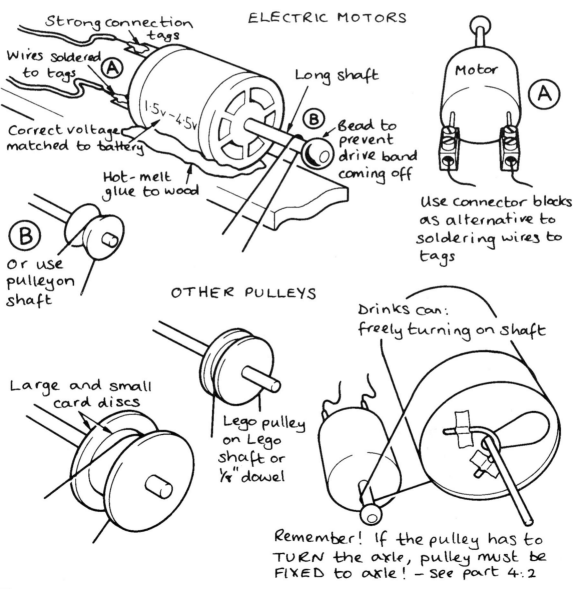

Fig.4

There are many ways of fixing a motor onto a model, e.g. Sellotape, pipe clips, plant ties, Blu-Tak, etc. The method we find most effective is to use hot glue. Whichever method you use, the motor must be fixed rigidly, with the shaft parallel to the axle, so that the elastic does not slip off.

Simple pulley systems

There are occasions when the use of the simple pulley arrangement illustrated here will not give sufficient speed reduction or increase in torque for the task it has to perform; when it is lifting a heavy weight, for example, or moving something very slowly. A series of pulleys may be used to reduce the speed and increase the torque further.

In this photograph, each axle is rotating about 15 times slower than the axle which drives it. The second axle is rotating at 15 x 15 times slower than the speed of the motor. The turning force of the second shaft is therefore 225 times larger than that of the motor and this increase in torque allows much greater weights to be lifted or moved by this axle. In practice, some slippage of the rubber bands will occur and so not all of this torque is usable. Using gearwheels instead of pulleys will prevent this slippage. Part 4:8 discusses how to use gears.

SUGGESTED READING

Energy in Primary Science. Department of Energy

4:8 USING GEARS

Almost all machines and domestic appliances use gears, although we rarely see them for they are hidden inside the housing. Some gears are easily seen, e.g. on guitars, hand-drills, salad-spinner, tin-openers and lever-action corkscrews. In each of these, the gears have a specific task to perform. Sometimes this is obvious: the salad-spinner gears are there to increase the rotation speed of the drum. Others are harder to analyse; the guitar machine-head gears have at least three different tasks to perform. These are described later in this section.

Children can learn a good deal about gears from observing and discussing the actions of gears in these everyday machines, once their attention is drawn to them. Encourage the children to look for gear systems when you are out on a visit. You will find examples in many places, e.g. canal wharfs and locks, mills and Victorian kitchens.

Whenever children are observing gears in operation, there are some fundamental ideas to draw out. Using construction kits these ideas can be explored with children throughout the primary age range. There are several good kits available for infant children which include large gearwheels which can be arranged to mesh together and form simple gear trains. Most of the large educational suppliers carry a wide range of kits suitable for different ages.

▶ *Functions of Gears*

The gears on a hand-drill perform two tasks:
- they make the drill bit turn more rapidly than your hand is turning;
- they change the direction of the movement from a vertical plane to a horizontal plane.

The gears on a manual egg whisk do the same job, and in addition drive two or three beaters at the same time. Notice how the gearing mechanism keeps the beaters from colliding with each other. Here, the gears are acting as a sort of timing system just as they do in a clock, another very common use for gears.

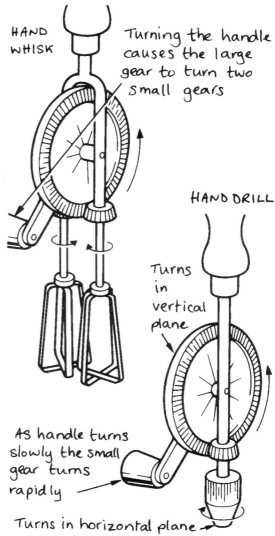

Fig.1 *Examples of gears*

Making a simple gear system

▶ Simple Gear Train

A simple gear train is one which has a single gearwheel on each turning shaft.

A simple gear train

Meshing of two gears of different sizes

Two gearwheels with equal numbers of teeth will turn in opposite directions when they mesh together. Their shafts will rotate at the same speed. In order to make these gears turn in the same direction, a third gearwheel needs to be introduced into the system.

In an arrangement where the two gears are of different sizes, the smaller gearwheel always turns faster than the bigger one. The difference in their speeds is determined by the ratio between the number of teeth on each of the gearwheels; the greater the difference in the number of teeth, the greater the difference in speed. When an eight-tooth gear meshes with a 40-tooth gear the smaller one has to turn five times to make the larger one turn once, i.e. a ratio of 5:1.

WORDS

'Cog' wheel means gear wheel. A cog is the old word for a tooth on a gear wheel

Introducing an idler into the gear system

Now, the two outer gears turn in the *same* direction and at the *same* speed. The size of the middle gear is unimportant. Its function is simply to make the two outer shafts turn in the same direction. This gear is called an idler.

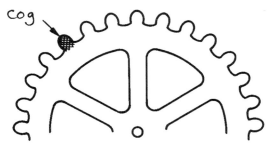

Fig.2

Windmills are particularly rich in gears and being so big and slow-moving, compared to most modern machinery, they clearly illustrate the different tasks that gears perform. The sails of the windmill turn a horizontal shaft. The stones are turned by a vertical shaft. Gears connect these two shafts together and turn the direction of drive through approximately 90 degrees.

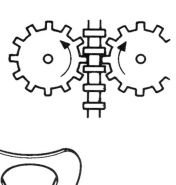

The sails turn rather slowly, not usually more than 10-12 revolutions per minute (rpm); the stone (the topstone is called the runner) needs to turn much more rapidly than this if it is to grind the corn successfully. The gearwheel fixed to the wind shaft is of a much larger diameter and has more teeth than the gearwheel attached to the upright shaft and as a result the runner turns more quickly than the sails.

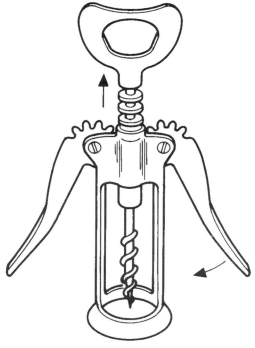

The gears on the corkscrew opposite are used to convert rotating motion (the arms swinging down) into linear motion (the cork pulling straight up). This mechanism can also work in the opposite direction, changing linear motion into rotary motion. The sluice paddle on a canal lock works this way.

▶ Worm Gear

Fig.3 *The gear mechanism on a bottle opener*

Guitar strings are tensioned with a worm and spur-gear arrangement. A worm gear, which looks like a thick screw, counts as a one-toothed gearwheel. When used with a 20-toothed gear, the ratio between them is 20:1. On the guitar, a large movement of the tuning peg creates a very small movement on the shaft that winds the string. This allows very fine adjustment of the tension in the strings for tuning.

Another feature of worm gears is that you cannot use another gear to drive the worm around, so the guitar string cannot unwind itself. This resistance to being driven makes worm gears safe to use in passenger lift systems, for example.

Worm gears on guitars

▶ Gear Boxes

It is often necessary to reduce the speed of rotation when small electric motors are being used as these usually run too rapidly to be connected directly to the working parts of a model. These motors turn fast but provide little turning force or torque (see Part 4:7). both of these problems are solved at once by using a simple gear train.

Compound gear train

Simple gear train

Gears provide a change of speed by exchanging speed for torque; when they reduce the speed, they increase the torque to the same degree. If the speed is reduced by five times, as in the above example, the torque will be increased by five times too. This is a complex idea and the best way to develop an understanding of it is to make up a simple gear train with a construction kit, such as Lego, and feel the differences in turning the shafts with your fingers.

A simple gear train does not always provide a sufficient change in speed or torque. In these instances, a compound gear train is required.

▶ Compound Gear Train

In a compound gear train, each shaft is linked to the next by gears arranged in pairs so that drive is transmitted from a small gear to a large gear. With each successive shaft, the reduction in speed is matched with a corresponding increase in torque.

The ratio between each pair of meshing gears is multiplied by the ratio of the next pair. This can give quite a large change both in speed and torque from the input shaft to the output shaft.

▶ Using Gears in Models

Children at Key Stages 1 and 2 are most likely to use gears when they are working with construction kits. A complete gear box can be made from a kit and fitted into a model as a unit. This is much more likely to be successful than trying to mount individual gear components into a model.

A model conveyer belt

Sometimes it is more convenient to use pulley systems (see Part 4:7) which do not demand such a high degree of precision in their positioning. If Lego motors are being used, a gear-block is available which simply push-fits onto the motor to provide the necessary speed reduction.

Making a gear box entirely from Lego can use up a lot of the components from a kit, and it is possible to combine Lego successfully with other materials in a number of ways. Packs of most of the components can be purchased separately to provide a 'top-up' supply for the kits.

Lego beams can be fixed with hot glue onto a model to provide the correct spacing for Lego axles. This reduces the amount of beams that need to be used.

It is also possible to obtain plastic gears which push-fit onto dowel. (See Part 4:5 for ways of fitting axles onto models.)

▶ Making Gears

It is possible for the children to make gears for themselves using a variety of readily available materials. For example, lolly sticks, match sticks or pieces of dowel can be set out radially on a card disc and covered by a second disc.

For gears to mesh together, it is essential that the spacing of the teeth is very accurate. Even when gears of different sizes mesh together the spaces between the teeth of both gears must still be the same. There are some simple jigs (holding devices) available from suppliers which help the children to achieve this accuracy.

Corrugated card on the rim of cheese boxes or lids can be fixed to a piece of board so that the ridges mesh with each other. This can demonstrate the way in which two gears meshing against one another will rotate in different directions.

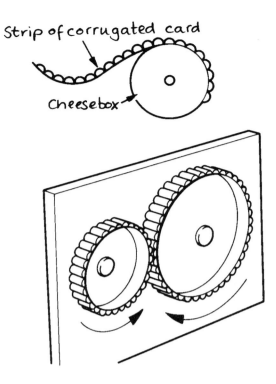

Fig .4 *Making your own gears*

Home-made gears are rarely accurate enough to work reliably in models but are useful for investigating simple operations. Beyond this level, construction kits are excellent for investigations.

Whenever a gear box is being constructed from materials other than kits, there are a number of things to be considered:
• accurate spacing of the axles is essential if the gears are to mesh. The axles must be parallel;
• the axles should be supported on both sides of the gearwheels to prevent them from bending, allowing the gearwheels to spring out of the mesh. Because bevel gears cannot be supported at each side, their shafts must be supported in at least two places (see Fig.5);
• the axle bearings must be made of low-friction materials (see Part 4:5) and the axle should not be too loose or the gears will disengage.

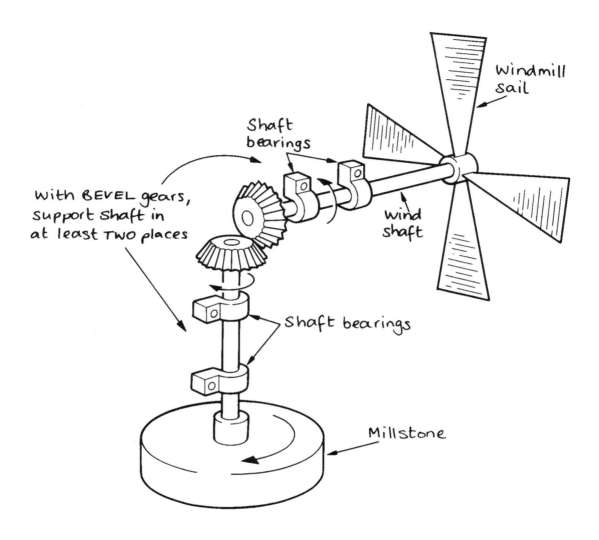

Fig .5 *The gear mechanism of a windmill*

4:9 PNEUMATICS AND HYDRAULICS

The idea of moving objects by using fluids (air or liquid) should be a familiar one. All around us are examples we can observe easily, e.g. the tip-up lorry, the extending ladder of a fire-engine, JCBs and other construction site machinery.

The basic principles of hydraulic and pneumatic movement are the same: movement is created at one end of a column of air (pneumatics) or liquid (hydraulics) and the pressure of the movement on the column of air or liquid is transmitted along its length creating movement at the opposite end (see Fig. 1).

When the piston at A is pressed, the column of air in the linking tube is compressed and the movement is transmitted along the tube resulting in movement of the piston at B. This is a simple pneumatic action. There may be a slight delay between the action at A and the reaction at B because of the compressibility of the air and the movement at B probably will not be quite as much as that at A for the same reason.

This same arrangement can be used to demonstrate a hydraulic operation if the syringes and tube are filled with water. Hydraulic systems on machines generally use a special oil which doesn't freeze or support the growth of algae as water does.

> **WARNING**: if the children are examining real hydraulic systems, make sure the children do not touch the oil as it can be toxic.

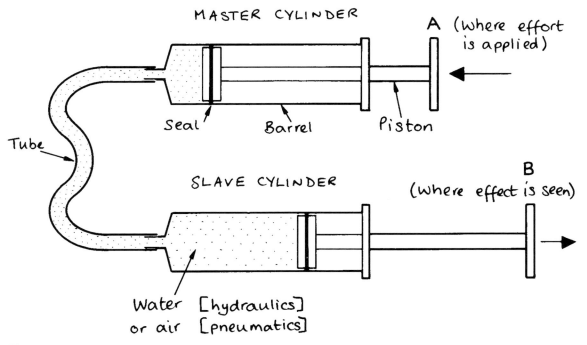

Fig .1

▶ Making a Hydraulic System

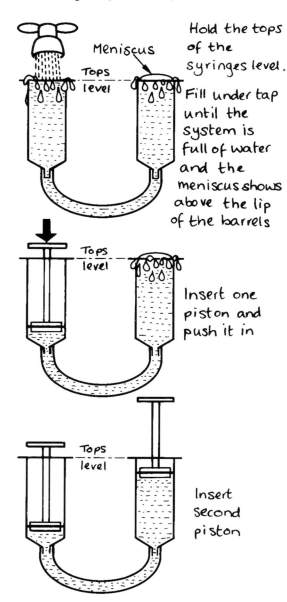

Fig.2 *Making a hydraulic system*

Keeping everything under water, fix one syringe to one end and push the piston right in, then fix the cylinder of the second syringe to the other end. Now push in the piston gently. The system is now assembled.

Now, when piston A is pressed, the reaction at B is equal and instantaneous because the liquid does not compress as does the air. In addition, the movement at B can be reversed by withdrawing the piston at A.

▶ Using Balloons to Create Movement

At Key Stage 1, the idea of moving things with air can be introduced by using a balloon and some means of inflating it. To make it easier to inflate, blow up the balloon a few times with an inflator to stretch it. The movement of the balloon as it inflates may be used to operate some part of a child's model.

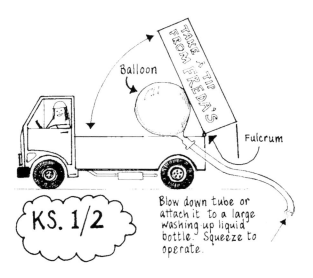

Air in the system spoils the efficiency of the hydraulic action because it compresses and so some of the input movement is lost.

An alternative method is to fill a bowl with water and into it put the tube and the dismantled syringes. If there are air bubbles remaining in the tube, suck water up through the tube until it is almost full then re-immerse the tube. (This overcomes the problem of internal resistance in the tube.)

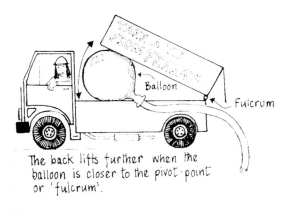

The back lifts further when the balloon is closer to the pivot-point or 'fulcrum'.

Fig.3

Here, the balloon lifts the back of a truck which is hinged with a simple card flap. The position of the balloon is very important. The nearer the hinge (i.e. the fulcrum) the greater the movement.

On a model, such as a truck, it would be difficult to conceal an inflator or plastic bottle, and it may be better to use a balloon fixed to some PVC tube (using PVC insulating tape) so that the tube can pass out of the rear of the vehicle and movement can be controlled from a distance.

Another simple application of this idea is to operate the jaws of an 'animal'. The balloon needs to be placed close to the hinge of the jaws for maximum efficiency. If fabric is used to create a body this will conceal the inflator.

OPENING MOUTHS KS.1

Fix balloon to bottle neck with electrician's tape or florist's wire.

Squeezy bottle   Balloon

Reinforce the hinge with card.

Fig.4

▶ One Input : Two Outputs

An interesting extension of balloon lifts is to power two balloons from the same air source so that two things lift at the same time; an arrangement that resembles a pair of lungs.

In the diagram, the wings of the bird are made to move using this idea. The wings are card flaps, hinged to the body of the model, and the balloons fixed so that they are close to the hinge. An air source concealed at the back of the bird inflates the balloons and the bird flaps its wings.

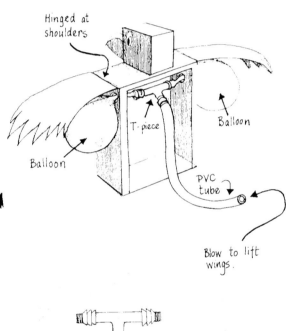

Hinged at shoulders

T-piece   Balloon

Balloon

PVC tube

Blow to lift wings.

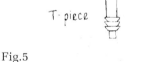

T-piece

Fig.5

For more experienced children, T-pieces can be built into hydraulic systems, too.

▶ Using Syringes to Create Movement

When syringes are used to create movement, the important considerations are how the syringe is to be fixed and how it is going to move. For example, to raise the tipper on a truck the slave cylinder may be fixed so that the piston moves vertically. As the tipper is lifted, the piston slides under its base.

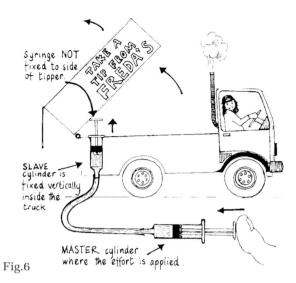

Syringe NOT fixed to side of tipper.

TAKE A TIP FROM FREDA'S

SLAVE cylinder is fixed vertically inside the truck.

MASTER cylinder where the effort is applied.

Fig.6

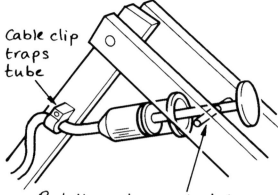

DIGGER ARM

Cable clip traps tube

Rod through wood strips and shaft of piston

Sometimes, the movement of the piston needs to be more controlled, for example, on a digger arm. The end of the piston and the base of the cylinder both need to pivot as the arm lifts or descends and the angles alter.

This can be achieved by fastening the PVC tube at the base of the cylinder to the model so that it acts as a hinge and attaching the end of the piston to an axle so that it pivots (see Fig. 7).

Fig.7

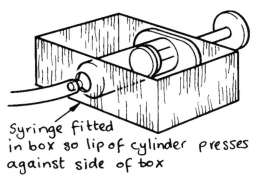

Syringe fitted
in box so lip of cylinder presses
against side of box

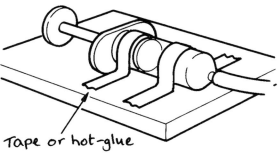

Tape or hot-glue

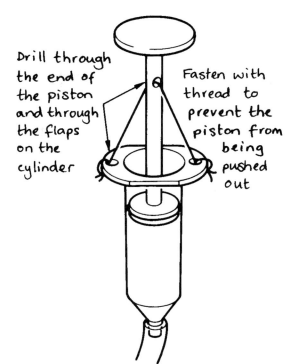

Drill through
the end of
the piston
and through
the flaps
on the
cylinder

Fasten with
thread to
prevent the
piston from
being
pushed
out

Fig.9

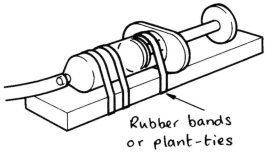

Rubber bands
or plant-ties

Fig.8

Sometimes, if you push too far on one piston of a hydraulic system the other piston will shoot out of the cylinder and the water will flood out onto the model. To avoid this you can limit the movement of the pistons (see Fig.9).

The slow, controlled movement of a syringe can be used effectively with levers to create movement. Thread linking the piston of a syringe with one end of a lever will allow the movement of the piston to activate the mechanism.

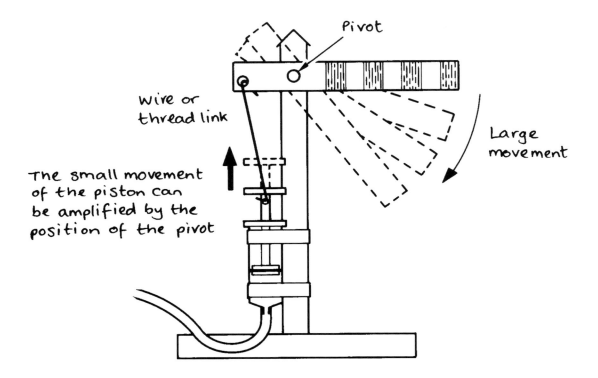

Pivot

wire or
thread link

The small movement
of the piston can
be amplified by the
position of the pivot

Large
movement

Fig.10

At Key Stage 1, this idea of using levers to amplify movement can be introduced without the syringes, simply pulling the thread.

▶ More Advanced Concepts

So far, we have referred to hydraulic systems which use two identical syringes to transfer movement. When the syringes are of different sizes the effect is rather different (see Fig. 11).

The large amount of movement of the 2 ml syringe creates a much smaller movement of the 10 ml syringe, and conversely the small amount of movement of the 10 ml syringe is amplified as the 2 ml syringe operates.

In gear systems, a decrease of speed is accompanied by an increase in torque (see Part 4:8). The decrease in movement of the large piston is similarly accompanied by an increase in its force.

These are both examples of 'mechanical advantage', i.e. these systems are being used to increase force.

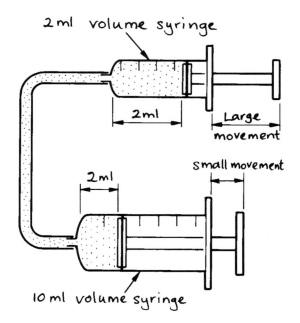

2ml volume syringe

2ml   Large movement

small movement

2ml

10 ml volume syringe

Small movement of LARGE syringe
causes
Large movement of SMALL syringe

Fig.11

98

4:10 USING COMPUTERS FOR CONTROL

The words 'computer controlled' are more and more often used now when describing the latest products of advanced technologies. When a machine (whether it is a city's traffic control system or a household washing machine) is controlled by a computer it is able to sense and respond to changes in the working environment. For example, the rates at which traffic is building up on different roads during rush hour is sensed and the various traffic lights altered to even out the queues. This sort of automatic control has been part of our technology for a long time but the appearance of cheap and powerful computers has made it all very much easier and more effective.

Some control devices are very simple, and need to be handled each time they do their job, for example, simple electrical light switches. Others are more complex and can continue to operate on their own once they are turned on, for example, central heating thermostats.

A model of Tower Bridge with a computerised control programme

Increasingly, teachers and children in primary schools are using their computers to control the models they have built. If you haven't seen it done, the thought of children connecting lights, motors and buzzers up to a computer may be rather daunting, but the equipment now available makes it all surprisingly easy.

Computers allow children to experience quite complex systems beyond what would be possible using simple electrical circuits.

When the children are using the computer for control in this way the important things they are learning are not about computers, but about control. Most computers can be used for control. The BBC and the Nimbus are most commonly used in schools, and control equipment (both hardware and software) is available for these machines. The following sections describe how you can connect up to your computer.

▶ BBC Computer

On the underside of the BBC computer, there are sockets which allow connections to be made to the computer. The printer or the disk drive may be plugged into one of these. The printer port allows signals to be sent from the computer in the form of electrical impulses, and it is these electrical signals, normally used to drive a printer, which can be used to drive components such as lights, buzzers and motors. The user port does not give out electrical signals but leads connecting the user port to sensors and switches of various kinds can feed information from the outside world into the computer; in other words, it can be used to monitor the environment.

▶ Nimbus Computer

If you are using a Nimbus you will need a BBC-style printer and user ports to connect up the control hardware. For some models, you will need to obtain a BBC extension port to plug into the back of the computer. Other models have a BBC-style extension port built in. If you need advice, consult your information technology centre.

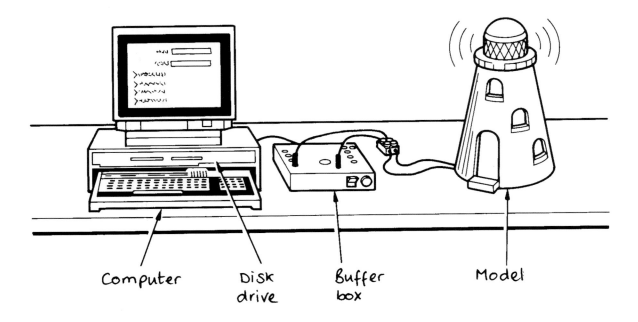

Fig.1 *Connecting a model to a computer using an interface (or buffer box)*

In order to use the facilities of the computer, connections have to be made to the ports and this is usually done by using an interface or buffer box. This is a box which plugs into the printer port, and usually the user port too. Components such as lights, buzzers, motors and switches can be plugged into this buffer box and controlled by the computer. The sockets on the buffer box which are used to turn on and off lights, buzzers and motors are referred to as the *outputs*, and the sockets into which sensors and switches are plugged are called the *inputs*.

The printer and user ports provide the facility to monitor eight outputs and eight inputs and most buffer boxes match this. Some buffer boxes only plug into the printer port, and if this is the case then the box will only have the facility to do eight operations. Usually, the software written for these boxes is arranged so that six outputs can be used and two sensors, and this will limit the work that you can do. If you buy one of these types of box, bear in mind also that they require specially written software and the choice available to you is more limited than for the eight-output, eight-input boxes.

As the name suggests, the buffer box protects the computer from damage which may be caused if any power is fed back accidently into the computer via the ports. It also allows you to provide a power source for components because the computer itself can supply only limited power. Some buffer boxes plug into the mains supply and provide a variable voltage. Others simply plug into the computer and batteries are connected to the box to provide the power needed to drive the components.

► Choosing an Interface

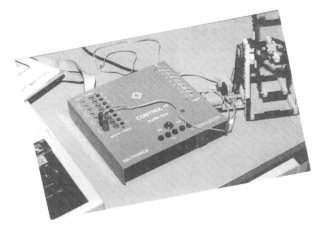

Interface box

There is a range of commercially produced interface boxes available for use in primary schools. Most interfaces have sockets for inputs and outputs, but some systems have separate boxes for the output and input devices, for example, the Cambridge In-Control interface.

Some important considerations when selecting interfaces are:
- safety for users. Is it fully insulated, fused and does it meet British Standard safety requirements?
- protection for the computer. Is the interface designed to prevent power being fed back accidently into your computer and damaging it?
- inputs and outputs. Does the interface give you a full eight-in / eight-out facility? Some, for example Lego, have only a six-output and two-input facility, and a single lead to the computer connects to the printer port;
- components. Is a range of output and input devices (e.g. switches, motors, lights, etc), prepared with appropriate plugs, available from the supplier? Is it easy to prepare plugs yourself? Jack plugs need wires soldered to them whilst the wires to 4 mm stackable plugs are fitted usually by screwing them down;
- power supply. Does the interface have a built-in power supply? This is a convenient way to power components but limits you to the voltage set by the box. Boxes without a built-in power supply need to be powered with batteries and this allows you to select a voltage that matches the components available in the classroom;
- cost. Prices range widely and you should shop around. An expensive box may provide only the same facilities as the cheaper ones. Boxes without a built-in power supply are cheaper.

► Software

There are a number of factors to consider when choosing software:
- software for use by children within the primary age range must not demand a high level of programming skills or too high a reading-age. It is usual for the command words (such as *switchon*, *switchoff* and *wait*) to be called up with the user defined keys and so they do not need typing in;
- a screen display which clearly shows the state (on or off) of all the inputs and outputs is essential. Some software has the option of hiding the inputs or outputs if required;
- a simple, easy to use editing facility is essential;
- control languages based on a Logo-type structure are particularly appropriate for young children, building on the experiences they will have gained using Logo for mathematical activities. They enable the children to break down the problem into small parts and build simple procedures to deal with each. Individual procedures then may be incorporated into a larger procedure;
- some software requires a Logo chip to be fitted to the computer (e.g. Controller, Control Logo, Lego Logo) whilst others do not (e.g. Contact).

▶ Output Devices

Most schools will have already a range of output devices which may be used with the computer, e.g. bulbs, buzzers, motors. The important thing to remember is that the voltage of the components must match the voltage delivered by the interface box, and as this varies between boxes, you will need to check it carefully.

Some interfaces require a 'relay box' to be attached to the output ports to enable motors to be reversed. These usually plug into two adjacent sockets and the commands to operate the motor will be addressed to both of them.

Other boxes with a built-in relay have a separate row of output sockets for motors, and this provides the facility to drive three or four motors in both directions.

▶ Input Devices

Input devices are switches of various kinds which make or break the flow of electrical current in the two wires which attach the switch to the computer. This can be as simple as the two bare wires coming together or a more complex electronic light-sensing switch such as a light-dependent resistor (LDR). The computer is able to sense whether the switch is open or closed. The switches, including the home-made ones, described in Part 4:6 can be used with the computer.

The computer's ability to respond to light-sensitive switches makes it easy for children to use these components in their electrical circuits and when used with the computer they add a new dimension to the children's work. For example, the LDR responds to changes in the light level; the lighter it becomes the more current flows until the computer registers a state of *on*. As conditions darken, less current flows until a stage is reached when the computer registers *off*. This device would be useful in a lighthouse project where a fall in the light level due to fog, for example, would require an alarm to be sounded.

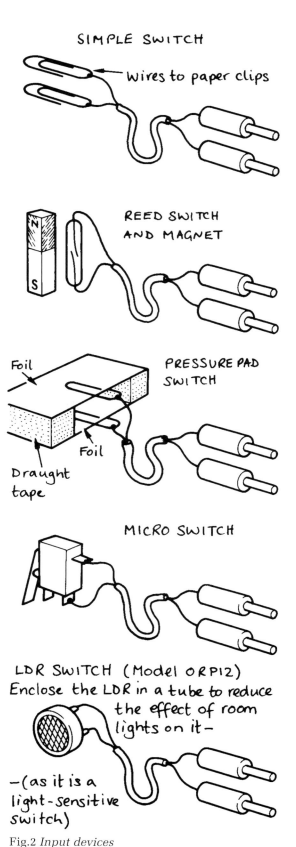

Fig.2 *Input devices*

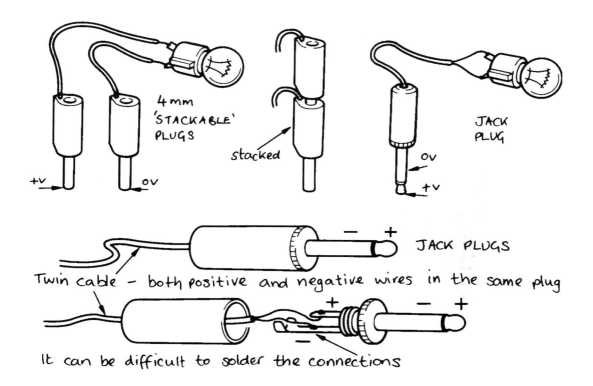

Fig.3 *Plugs*

Many buffer boxes can be purchased with a range of input and output devices fixed onto jack plugs which will fit the box, but it is often much cheaper to provide your own. A good supply of plugs with about 50 cm of cable fitted to each and terminating with bare leads may be prepared, and children can connect these using connector blocks to whatever devices they have used on their models.

Stackable plugs are the easiest plugs to deal with because some kinds don't need soldering; the wire simply screws into the plug. Since each component will need two wires, a positive and a negative, it is a good idea to use the extra-flexible double cable and attach a red and a black plug to indicate the different polarity.

Some interfaces require components to be fitted to a twin-wire lead connected to a single jack plug. This may obsure the children's understanding that there is a positive and negative connection to the component, but has the advantage that there are less wires.

Jack plugs, which come in several sizes, are more difficult to connect wires to. Both the positive and the negative leads are connected to a single plug; these leads need soldering on with great care.

► *Connecting Models to a Computer*

It is possible to buy floor turtles, buggies and robotics kits which introduce children to computer control, but children can connect to the computer the models they have made which incorporate electrical circuits.

When children want to link their models to the computer, each component should be wired to a connector block in an easily accessible position, and labelled. The lead from the buffer box can then be wired into the same connectors to make the link between the computer and the components.

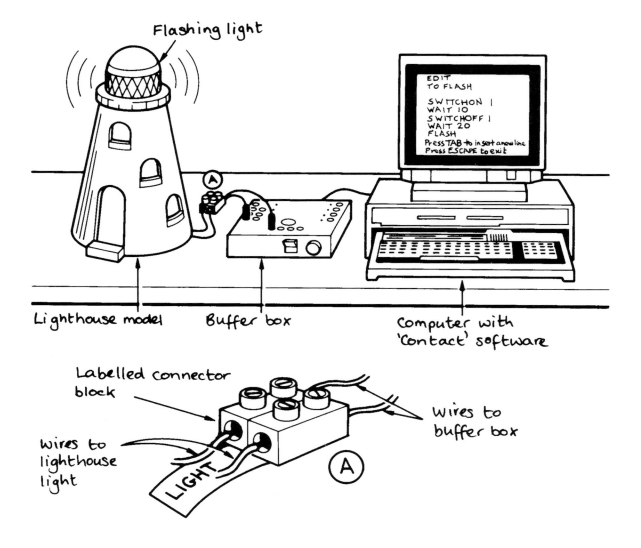

Flashing light

EDIT
TO FLASH

SWITCHON 1
WAIT 10
SWITCHOFF 1
WAIT 20
FLASH
Press TAB to insert a new line
Press ESCAPE to exit

Lighthouse model   Buffer box   Computer with 'Contact' software

Labelled connector block

wires to lighthouse light

LIGHT

Wires to buffer box

Ⓐ

Fig.4 *Using the computer for control*

If you have several models that are to be linked to the computer, only the leads to the buffer box need to be disconnected and re-used. Providing the leads to the components are labelled with the number of the socket they were connected to, it is a simple matter to re-connect the model to the buffer box on another occasion.

▶ **Getting Started**

Although computers can perform sophisticated control functions, a first step for children might be to link the computer to a model they have made which incorporates a light or buzzer, and to introduce them to the commands that turn these on and off.

As the children gain confidence they learn quickly how to edit procedures so that lights can flash, two things can work at the same time or a procedure can be repeated a certain number of times. The use of the computer for control should parallel children's experiences in electrics, and progress alongside it.

▶ *Planning Sequences*

When the children begin to use complex sequences where several different operations are intended, they should be encouraged to plan the sequence of operations before creating the programme. There are several ways of approaching this.

Flowcharts

Flowcharts can help to clarify the order in which events happen. For example, at a level crossing barrier the following sequence might be identified:

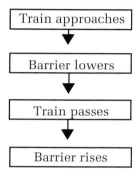

Fig.5 *A flowchart showing the sequence of events at a level crossing barrier*

Flowcharts help you to break the problem down into identifiable pieces, each of which might become a short procedure. Each of these can be tested and corrected before being built into a master programme which calls each procedure in the correct sequence.

Timelines

Timelines are helpful when several different operations are going on at the same time, as in traffic lights, for example (see Fig. 6).

> Switchon 3
> Wait *
> Switchoff 3
> Switchon 2
> Wait *
> Switchoff 2
> Switchon 1
> Wait *
> Switchon 2
> Wait *
> Switchoff 1 2

* Times needs to be inserted here. This is best done by observing a traffic light sequence and recording the length of time each light remains on. This procedure can be edited so that the sequence will repeat itself.

Fig. 6 *A timeline showing the sequence of events at traffic lights*

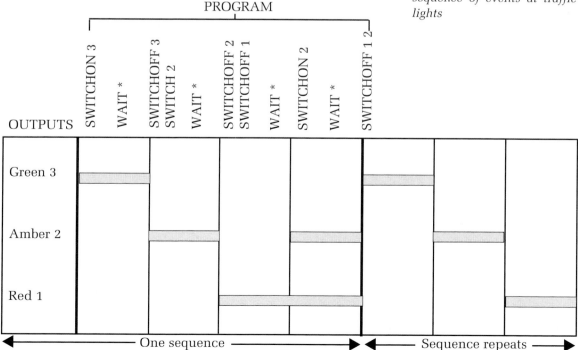

Whatever method is used, and children may invent their own, the aim is to clarify the order in which things are to happen. The need for this will be clear if you ask the children to describe a traffic light sequence for you; they will need to observe and time one at first hand to get it right.

Using computers in this way, children gain powerful insights into the increasingly important role of the computer in our society and hence broaden their understanding of control technology. Ordering their thoughts and expressing them in clear logical statements is essential for success. Children are highly motivated by seeing the results of their command of the computer being demonstrated in so concrete a fashion.

SUGGESTED READING

Primary Technology: the place of computer control 1989. Available from: NCET. University of Warwick Science Park, Coventry CV4 7EZ

TOOLS FOR DESIGN AND TECHNOLOGY

▶ Tools for Construction Activities

We have found that the set of tools you need is quite small and inexpensive and ideally each classroom should have a selection of basic tools.

As well as the tools in each class (or group of classes) there could be a kit of tools needed only occasionally, and tools only adults may use, which forms part of a shared school resource. Tools we would recommend include the following:

junior hacksaw
bench hook
utility snips
hammer
small hand-drill and twist drill
punch
card drill
safety paper cutters
craft knife and safety rule *
G-clamp
hole punch
hand reamer
hot-glue gun *

For a central resource:
tube-cutter *
drill and stand
coping saw
gents saw
small pliers

For electrical work:
automatic wire-stripper
electrical screwdriver
soldering iron and stand. *
* for teachers use only

Some schools have purchased a shaper saw for cutting sheet material. This is a more sophisticated and expensive tool and should not be regarded as essential.

▶ Storing Tools

There are many satisfactory ways of storing tools. Workers seem to fall into two categories: those who put each tool back where it belongs in the box or on the rack after using it, and those who leave each tool lying where it was last used but nevertheless know just where each one is. Both systems seem to work well enough for individuals in their own workroom, but the second one is definitely not available as an option for classrooms.

Some schools use tidy boxes, but this system makes it difficult to check for missing equipment. Scrabbling through the tools for those small items which naturally migrate to the bottom can damage tools and fingers. Drawers and trays in which each kind of tool has its own marked place are better.

The best system probably is one which uses a shadow board on which each tool's place and name is clearly shown. Missing items are easily noticed. The board can stand out on display, hook onto the wall or be put away in the cupboard.

Whatever system you adopt, make sure that the tools do not find themselves heaped into a box in the back of a cupboard where no-one can see them and no-one will use them.

▶ Tools for Working with Textiles

sewing machine, iron and ironing board or table felt for ironing on weaving cards hand loom specialist scissors: for cutting fabric, pinking shears, embroidery scissors sewing hoops: for keeping fabric taut whilst it is being decorated
knitting needles
sewing needles
crewel for embroidery, tapestry needles, bodkins, pins

unpicker: for unpicking stitches quickly and easily
measuring tapes
crochet hooks
carders and spindles for creating yarns from fleece.

▶ Tools for Working with Food

cooking facility: hot plate, cooker, microwave
kettle
timer
food processor or liquidiser and hand-mixer
saucepans
cutlery and other kitchen utensils
crockery: unbreakable
mixing bowls: unbreakable
tin opener
sieves
scales
baking tins: teflon finish are easiest to manage

peeler: left and right handed
chopping and cutting boards: melamine are most hygienic
pastry cutters
lemon squeezer
equipment for washing up.

▶ Art and Graphics Equipment

spray diffuser: simple tube device used to spray thin inks or paint over a surface to create a splatter effect,
letter stencils
printing materials: perspex sheet for rolling out inks, rollers
screen printing kit
drawing equipment: compass, set-square, protractor, dividers
rubber gloves: for use with dyes
camera.

CLASSROOM RESOURCES: CONSUMABLES

In this section we focus on consumables which have specific uses in design and technology activities. We assume schools will already have everyday materials such as powder paint, wax and pencil crayons and Plasticine. This is not an exhaustive list but might provide a basis for selecting resources to meet your needs.

▶ Small Components for Construction Work

These items may be stored in yoghurt pots, or similar, in a tray where they are accessible to the children. It is the range of items that is important rather than the quantity.

paper fasteners: 13 mm useful for making
  battery boxes
  paper clips
  drawing pins
  straight pins
  Blu-Tak
  beads
  marbles
  candles
electrical cable-clips: 7 mm for use with 5 mm
  dowel
panel pins: 5/8 for use with cable clips on 8 mm
  wood
foam draught excluder
washers
thread: extra strong as well as normal strength
cotton reels
elastic bands
card discs.

▶ Adhesive Tape

Sellotape
paper parcel tape: can easily be painted over
security tape: metallic, conducting tape used
  in security systems
double sided tape
insulating tape.

▶ Adhesives

PVA: can be used safely with wood and card
hot glue: will glue plastics and metal but
  should only be used by the teacher or with
  older children under direct supervision
fabric glues: **note** will not wash out of
  clothes
semi-solid adhesive sticks (like Pritt): particularly useful for small children working
  with card and paper
cold water paste: cellulose or starch-based,
  useful for papier-mâché.

▶ Electrical

bulbs (MES)
bulb holders: nylon clip-on type are better
  than batton
buzzers
motors: buy high-torque motors
LEDs with resistor: useful for top of age
  range
battery boxes
multi-strand wire: 7/0.2 is a useful gauge
connector strip: for joining wires
reed switches and magnets.

▶ Hydraulics and Pneumatics

balloons
balloon inflator
PVC tube: inside diameter 5 mm
syringes: 5 ml and 10 ml will probably be
  sufficient. Choose syringes with a neoprene
  seal. Those without do not work as well
PVC tube to fit the syringes
T-pieces.

▶ Wood

dowel: ply wheels are often pre-drilled to push-fit onto 5 mm dowel. It may be useful to have other sizes available, in smaller quantities

square section wood strip: 8 mm is ideal for constructing space frames, but a selection of other sizes is useful. The methods of constructing with this material are rather sophisticated for infants.

selection of other sections of wood: a pack of mixed sections is available from a number of suppliers and schools might find it useful to purchase one of these

wheels: ply, pre-drilled with a 5 mm hole in a variety of sizes.

▶ Metals

welding rod: 1/8" is useful for axles
aluminium foil baking dishes: for switches.

▶ Textiles

fabrics: printing fabric, calico, binca, felts, embroidery fabric, poplin, nets
kapok

offcut packs: fabrics, lace, elastic, woollen yarns
threads: for embroidery and sewing, metallic for decorative uses, wool, raffia
chalk: for outlining designs
fasteners: buttons, press-studs, hooks and eyes
velco
zips
sequins
beads.

▶ Graphic Media

Most classrooms will have a good range of materials. These suggestions may extend the range of media provided:

fabric paints, dyes and crayons
printing inks: for block and screen
Brusho: comes in a range of strong colours and can be used with a spray diffuser, to dye fabrics and to achieve many other interesting effects
paints: powder, ready-mix paints, watercolour, fluorescent
drawing pencils: a range especially of soft grades such as B and 2B
masking tape
fibre or felt pens.

SUPPLIERS

▶ General Resources

It is worth shopping around for the resources you need; prices and delivery times vary widely. Some LEAs have local buying agencies which sell at very competitive prices; don't forget to check these out.

Teaching Technology Systems Ltd
Unit 4, Holmewood Fields Business Park
Park Road
Chesterfield S42 5UY
Tel: 0246 850085

Sheffield Purchasing Organisation (SPO)
Staniforth Road
Sheffield S9 3GZ
Tel: 0742 560424

Heron Educational Ltd
Unit 3
Carrwood House
Carrwood Road
Sheepbridge
Chesterfield S41 9QB
Tel: 0246 453354

Nestec Ltd
Unit 24D
North Tyne Industrial Estate
Whitley Road
Long Benton
Newcastle upon Tyne NE12 9SZ
Tel: 091 266 3959

Yorkshire Purchasing Organisation
Park Lodge Lane
Wakefield WF1 4JR
Tel: 0924 367272

Trylon Ltd
Thrift Street
Wollaston
Northants NN9 7QJ
Tel: 0933 664275

Nottingham Educational Supplies
Ludlow Hill Road
West Bridgford
Nottingham NG2 6HD
Tel: 0602 234251

▶ Wood

Porters of Selby
Station Road
Selby
N. Yorks Y08 0NP
Tel: 0757 708709

▶ Electrics

Surplus Buying Agency
Birley School
Fox Lane
Sheffield S12 4WU
Tel: 0742 646186

JPR Electronics
Unit M
Kingsway Ind. Estate
Kingsway
Luton
Beds LU1 1LP
Tel: 0582 410055

Elf Educational Services
32 Aragon Drive
Ilford
Essex I96 2TS
Tel: 01 500 3254

Rapid Electronics
Heckworth Close
Severalls Industrial Estate
Colchester
Essex CO4 4TB
Tel: 0206 751 166

▶ Soft Materials

Craftpacks
Orchard Farm
33 Lower Church Road
Titchfield Common
Fareham
Hants PO14 4PW
Tel: 048957 2198

▶ *Computer Hardware and Software*

Control interfaces
Cambridge Microtech (Control IT)
Westmead
28 Ansley Way
St Ives
Huntingdon PE17 4SN
Tel: 0480 66141

Deltronics
91 Heol-Y-Parc
Cefneithin
Dyfed SA14 7DL
Tel: 0269 843728

Phobox Electronics
Holworth House
Holworth
Dorchester
Dorset DT2 8NJ

Controller (BBC & NIMBUS)
NCET Publications
Hoddle Doyle & Meadows Ltd
Old Mead Road
Elsenham
Bishop's Stortford
Herts CM22 6NJ

Lego Control Logo
Lego UK Ltd
Rutin Rd
Wrexham
Clywd
Tel: 0305 853767

Control Software
1. Contact (BBC)
Resource
Coventry Grove
Off Exeter Road
Doncaster DN2 4PY
Tel: 0302 340331

2. Control Logo (BBC)
Logotron
Dales Brewery
Gwydir Street
Cambridge CB1 2LJ
Tel: 0223 323656

ADHESIVES

▶ PVA

By far the most useful, cheapest and safest adhesive is white PVA 'school' glue. It will join absorbent materials (e.g. paper, card, wood, fabrics, and pottery with unglazed surfaces) very strongly indeed; often stronger than the original material. It will not join plastics or metals, unfortunately. It does take a while to dry, which can be frustrating, but this can be minimised if it is used thinly rather than thickly since the actual working thickness of glue is extremely thin, the rest being mostly water which has to dry off. Teach your children to apply the adhesive thinly and evenly over the whole of the surface to be joined, not just to blob it on. A paint brush is a better applicator than a spatula for this reason.

PVA is soluble, making it useful when recycling the timber in scrapped projects by soaking in water until the glue dissolves. PVA will not fill gaps, so surfaces to be joined should be held tightly together with fingers, elastic bands, paper clips, under weights or in G-clamps.

▶ Hot-melt Glue (Glue Gun)

Although potentially injurious and not cheap, this glue is invaluable for its ability to stick almost anything and for the speed with which it sets. In fact it sets so rapidly that there is no time for adjustments to be made and sometimes the quality and neatness of the work suffers. It is particularly useful for joining those materials which PVA cannot, i.e. non-absorbent materials such as plastics and metals. Unlike PVA which sets hard, hot-melt glue sets as flexible as the original glue stick, making it unsuitable for making rigid structures.

▶ Rubber Solutions

These are not useful in construction because they set into a flexible layer.

▶ Superglues

These expensive and specialised adhesives can be extremely useful but their ability to stick human skin together makes them unsuitable for children's use. Without believing everything the advertisements claim, they will do some remarkable things. For example, turning a rubber band into a Möbius loop.

▶ Contact Adhesives

These glues work on non-absorbent surfaces such as plastics. Although powerful, they are difficult to use correctly and most of them are solvent-based and give off strong fumes. They are messy adhesives and any spillages on clothes would be impossible to remove. For all these reasons they are *not* to be recommended for primary school use.

▶ Epoxy-resins

These are enormously strong adhesives, the best known of which is perhaps Araldite. They come in two parts, adhesive and hardner, which must be mixed together. This starts a rapid catalytic reaction and within a few minutes the glue has set hard. They are expensive adhesives, but very useful for teachers to use.

▶ Fabric Adhesives

These adhesives are particularly useful for collage and applique work but do not wash out of clothing and therefore need to be used very carefully. They are, sometimes, not recommended for use by primary children.

▶ Cold-water Pastes

Use only those which are specifically recommended for use by primary children and you will avoid the problem of harmful additives.

▶ Pritt Type Glues

These solid sticks of glue are easy for small children to handle and can be less messy. They are particularly useful for work with paper and card.

▶ Adhesive Tapes

A range of adhesive tapes is helpful to have available. They are useful for quick fixing. You might be able to provide the following:

Sellotape: works well on plastic sheets for kites but unsticks quickly when wet

double-sided tape

masking or drafting tape: peels off drawing paper without tearing

insulating tape: available in a range of pretty colours

paper parcel tape: inexpensive and takes paint well

conducting tape: adhesive foil tape useful in some electrical work.

APPENDIX FIVE

RECORDING CHILDREN'S EXPERIENCE IN DESIGN AND TECHNOLOGY

In Part 2, we suggested that more than one kind of record would be needed to plan for breadth and balance in design and technology activities. Here, we suggest some approaches to use for organising these records.

Recording systems must inform you of each child's level of attainment in each attainment target and the areas of the programmes of study covered by their activities.

To help you develop a school record system we offer the following three record formats as a starting point for discussion:

- recording attainment targets;
- pupil's record;
- recording experience.

▶ Recording Attainment Targets

You will need to record the actual level of attainment within each attainment target for each child. See sheet 1, page 118

There are many systems available for recording a child's level of attainment. Some are in the form of a grid with a box for each statement of attainment for each level and for each attainment target. A problem with such a system is that the number of statements is so numerous that it is impossible to remember what they are without continually referring back to the order. We suggest that all the relevant statements of attainment from Attainment Targets 1 to 4 are photocopied from the order and reorganised for ease of reference: for example, grouping by level of attainment.

Although a child may tend to do better at some aspects of the work than others (for example, be more capable of making things than developing designs) design and technology capability is concerned with the whole process across all four of the attainment targets for design and technology.

When a child has achieved competency in all four attainment targets at a particular level, a general comment from the teacher about the child's abilities might be included in the record.

▶ Pupil's Record

This record can be maintained by each child on completion of their design and technology project. It asks for information about their work at each stage of the process as defined by the attainment targets. It also provides the teacher with more precise details of the child's activity than the record of achievement. See sheet 2, page 119.

Future teachers will need to know which topics have been covered and what the children have actually made. They should be able to infer the National Curriculum context from this information, although you might decide to add this information to the sheet.

This format could be stored on computer so that the children can develop their language and word-processing skills as it is completed to produce a concise and informative text.

For children at Key Stage 1, this record may need to be simplified or completed by the teacher. The information on this sheet will help in the completion of recording the pupils' experience.

▶ Recording Experience

The information on sheets 3 and 4, pages 120 and 121, is organised under the four categories of the programmes of study. Under each category are general headings which indicate the range of experiences the children should meet. This is intended to focus in on what the children actually do.

The statements in the programmes of study are too general to be useful in recording actual work done or in planning particular activities. (For example, "explore and use a variety of materials to make things", Key Stage 1: Working with Materials.)

We have translated the broad general statements of the programmes of study into more specific areas of experience. Teachers will need to be familiar with the detail of the programmes of study in order to recognise the relationship between them and this record.

Schools may wish to alter the record to reflect their individual preferences. The range of experiences on this record is intended to help monitor the balance of children's design and technology experiences. Progression should be indicated in the teachers' comments as they complete the record.

Some aspects of the programmes of study are inherent in the teaching of design and technology and so do not appear as separate items on the record. Safety, for example, should be a part of learning how to use new materials and tools, whilst economic use of materials will be encouraged right across the curriculum. Aesthetic values will be discussed during the evaluation of both bought articles and the children's own work.

▶ Keeping the Record

The record provides a framework for teachers' comments about the children's learning. One record would need to be kept for each child. On completion of a design and technology task, the teachers should record the learning that has taken place. The balance across the range of experiences described in each of the four sections should be achieved over the Key Stage rather than the year. See sheet 5, page 122.

At Key Stage 1, when design and technology activities are likely to be more numerous and of shorter duration, it might be appropriate to fill in the record only when new areas of experience are met or when a step in understanding is achieved.

It is not intended that comments should be lengthy but that they should inform teachers and their colleagues of significant learning experiences.

▶ Explanatory Notes for Recording Experience

Using and Controlling Energy

human: pulling along or hand-winding a model

gravity: vehicle rolling down a slope; using a falling mass attached to a string to pull a vehicle along; unwinding to turn a shaft

wind/water: related through their traditional uses, i.e. driving mills, etc, though water power is really gravity. Wind now used to power boats, mills and aerogenerators

strain: this is the energy stored in a stretched rubber band or wound clockwork spring. The energy is usually put into the strained material by human muscles

electrical control : progression in electrical control begins with simple circuits without a switch powering one 'output', e.g. a light or a buzzer; to making and using simple on/off switches; to circuits with more than one 'output' when the differences between series and parallel arise; to motor-control circuits where the polarity must be control led

computer control: may progress through use of outputs; to use of inputs; to more complex control procedures. Computer control should not be regarded as a high-level version of electrical control, but as a parallel experience.

Moving Things

wheels and axles: control of friction and stability to ensure free-running. An axle can be connected to a power source such as stretched rubber or an electric motor. The latter will often require 'stepping down' with pulleys or gears to reduce the speed and increase the turning force

pulleys and gears: progression from simple pulleys, and gear trains of equal sized gears changing direction of rotation; to turning drive through an angle, usually 90 degrees; to different sizes of gears in order to change speed/force; to compound gear trains with two gears on some shafts to obtain high ratios

levers and linkages: progression from use of equal length arms; to unequal arms to change distance/force; to linked levers, crank/slider and other compound movements

hydraulics and pneumatics: progression from using balloons to produce movement; to use of syringes.

Working with Materials

textiles: using textiles for aesthetic purposes, for example, collage, is not necessarily design and technology but develops skills in this material

food : consideration of nutrition; appearance; taste and economy should be included in their activities

construction materials : card and timber can both be used in simple and complex ways, but most metals and plastics do not lend themselves to simple use. 3-D constructions in any material demand attention to stiffness and stability in addition to the problems of cutting to size and joining

graphic media: include the range of activities from simple mark-making tools such as pencils, paints and crayons to printing techniques for communicating ideas and enhancing the appearance of work.

Developing and Communicating Ideas

Spoken descriptions using correct technical words or expressions and researching ideas to help with design construction kits provide sequenced pictures which children at Key Stage 1 can use.

Simple outline shapes can be drawn on squared paper when planning constructions; progressing from 2-D showing only approximate shapes to scaled drawings and 3-D representations. A range of computer software is suitable for children to use for designing, e.g. Logo.

The ability to work cooperatively with other children sharing tasks to take account of different abilities.

Progression from saying what they're going to do next to planning a flow diagram of the expected sequence of stages they will go through.

Satisfying Needs and Addressing Opportunities

Progression will be from work dictated by personal interests; to identifying and responding to those of other people from simple valuations(i.e. does it work?); to an analysis of the relative success of different, conflicting demands of the design, and statements of how improvements can be made.

Awareness of both the positive and negative effects of technological products and their uses. (For example, the convenience of take-away food outlets and the litter that occurs in their vicinity; the unequal distribution of the benefits of technology between first and third world countries.)

Name:_____

Level 1

COMMENTS:

AT1
Identifying needs & opportunities

Pupils should be able to:
1a) describe to others what they have seen in familiar surroundings or visualised about imaginary situations.
1b) suggest what might be done.

AT2
Generating a design

Pupils should be able to:
1a) express their ideas about what they might do to meet an identified need or opportunity.

AT3
Planning and making

Pupils should be able to:
1a) use a variety of materials and equipment to make simple things.

AT4
Evaluating

Pupils should be able to:
1a) describe to others what they have done and how well they have done it.
1b) describe to others what they like and dislike about familiar artefacts, systems or environments.

Level 2

AT1
Identifying needs & opportunities

a) describe what they have observed or visualised and found out in their exploration.

Design and Technology Project Report

Name : _____   Date : _____

Topic : _____

Partners : _____

AT1

Describe what you made.

How did you get the idea ?

AT2

What plans did you make ?

AT3

What did you make it from ?

Describe how it was made.

AT4

Did it turn out as you wanted ?

What new things did you learn ?

	TASK	Moving picture or nursery rhyme	Sandwich	Cart for teddy	Very hungry caterpillar

TEACHER : Miss Comish	DEVELOPING AND USING ARTEFACTS, SYSTEMS AND ENVIRONMENTS
	
	Using and controlling energy
	* human
	* pull of gravity
	* wind/water
	* strain
	* electrical
	
	Computer control
	* outputs
	* inputs
	
	Moving things
	* wheels and axles:
	  free-wheeling
	  driven wheel/axle
	* pulleys:
	  simple trains
	  compound trains
	* gears:
	  simple trains
	  compound trains
	* levers and linkages
	* hydraulics and pneumatics:
	  balloons
	  syringes
		Spider pulled up spout with string
		
		Pivotted lever arm showing sun / moon. Used paper fastener
				Pull a long (slid!)
				
				Stuck on wheels
					Moved each day to a new food

YEAR 1	WORKING WITH MATERIALS
	
	* textiles:
	  knitting
	  sewing
	  weaving
	* food:
	  preparing uncooked
	  cooking
	* construction materials:
	  kits
	  recycled
	  card
	  wood
	  metals
	  plastics
	* graphic media:
	  printing
	  dyeing
	  IT
		Spider made from felt. Simple running stitch
		
		Cutting out
		-card
		-felt
			Spreading marg on bread	Used cereal box and stick on plastic lids with tape. Shown how to make wheels turn with fastener	Each card segment joined by a different method
					- string
					-paper fastener
					- staples. Talked about caterpillar food

NAME : Eileen Rose	DEVELOPING AND COMMUNICATING IDEAS * describe what they intend to do * use pictures and other references * work from plans (e.g. Lego) * draw plans and modify them * use IT when planning	Describe to me what the picture would do		Talked about how wheels turn	Decided together what to do
	SATISFYING NEEDS AND ADDRESSING OPPORTUNITIES * decide for themselves what to make * when designing for others, ask their preferences * evaluate outcome against original intention * make critical judgements about technology and its impact on our lives	Chose their favourite rhyme	Class chart about favourite sandwich. Chose filling from four choices	Chose a box big enough to fit teddy	Discussed which joining method best. Staples did not pivot

120

	TASK	Parkin	Christmas card	Theatre	Story book for Class 2

TEACHER : Mr Guy	DEVELOPING AND USING ARTEFACTS, SYSTEMS AND ENVIRONMENTS
	
	Using and controlling energy
	* human
	* pull of gravity
	* wind/water
	* strain
	* electrical
	
	Computer control
	* outputs
	* inputs
	
	Moving things
	* wheels and axles:
	  free-wheeling
	  driven wheel/axle
	* pulleys:
	  simple trains
	  compound trains
	* gears:
	  simple trains
	  compound trains
	* levers and linkages
	* hydraulics and pneumatics:
	  balloons
	  syringes
			Pop-up movement	Motorised curtain winder
				
				Used lego to make box
					Moving book with lift-up flaps, windows and rotating discs

YEAR 6	WORKING WITH MATERIALS
	
	* textiles:
	  knitting
	  sewing
	  weaving
	* food:
	  preparing uncooked
	  cooking
	* construction materials:
	  kits
	  recycled
	  card
	  wood
	  metals
	  plastics
	* graphic media:
	  printing
	  dyeing
	  IT
		Weighing and measuring ingredients. Used the food mixer	Used card, coloured inks and glitter	Made curtain and turned a hem by hand. Potato printing	Word processor and paint-spa

NAME : Andrew Hault	DEVELOPING AND COMMUNICATING IDEAS * describe what they intend to do * use pictures and other references * work from plans (e.g. Lego) * draw plans and modify them * use IT when planning	Chose recipe at home	Tried out ideas on scrap card	Worked in a group and planned together	Tried out many ideas before final book put together
	SATISFYING NEEDS AND ADDRESSING OPPORTUNITIES * decide for themselves what to make * when designing for others, ask their preferences * evaluate outcome against original intention * make critical judgements about technology and its impact on our lives	Discussed food for bonfire night. Class tasting session	Looked at bought cards and saw how to create movement	Performed a story for the class	Researched kinds of books suitable for Class 2

Name: _____

DEVELOPING AND USING ARTEFACTS,
SYSTEMS AND ENVIRONMENTS

YEAR

	1	2	3	4	5	6

Using and controlling energy
* human
* pull of gravity
* wind/water
* strain
* electrical

Computer control
* outputs
* inputs

Moving things
* wheels and axles:
  free-wheeling
  driven wheel/axle
* pulleys:
  simple trains
  compound trains
* gears:
  simple trains
  compound trains
* levers and linkages
* hydraulics and pneumatics:
  balloons
  syringes

WORKING WITH MATERIALS

* textiles:
  knitting
  sewing
  weaving
* food:
  preparing uncooked
  cooking
* construction materials:
  kits
  recycled
  card
  wood
  metals
  plastics
* graphic media:
  printing
  dyeing
  IT

DEVELOPING AND COMMUNICATING IDEAS

* describe what they intend to do
* use pictures and other references
* work from plans (e.g. Lego)
* draw plans and modify them
* use IT when planning

SATISFYING NEEDS AND
ADDRESSING OPPORTUNITIES

* decide for themselves what to make
* when designing for others, ask their
  preferences
* evaluate outcome against
  original intention
* make critical judgements about
  technology and its impact on our
  lives

INDEX